'*Synergy* is a thoughtful, thorough approach to an opportunity that has long eluded many corporations. The authors use their considerable experience to create practical tools for managers at both corporate centers and business units, showing how the whole can truly become more valuable than the sum of the parts.'

Rosabeth Moss Kanter
Harvard Business School,
author of *Rosabeth Moss Kanter on the Frontiers of Management*

'Campbell and Goold have done it again. *Synergy* is going to be as important as "*Corporate-Level Strategy*". I have ordered copies for my Top 100 managers.'

Belmiro de Azevedo
President, Sonae Investimentos

'As in their previous work on the role of the corporate centre, Andrew Campbell and Michael Goold have taken on one of the great sacred cows of conglomerate strategy – "synergy" – and subjected it to a detailed, rational analysis. The mental disciplines and analytical tools they offer shed new light on a critical yet misunderstood area of management.'

Ken Whitton
Director of Strategy Development, Kingfisher

'For those of us who strive for synergy, this book is full of gold. If managers read no further than the section on four mental biases, they will gain significant value. But there is much more: the examples are frighteningly relevant; the thinking disciplines are essential for any decision maker; and the tools are practical. A book for the bestseller list.'

Bill Newby
Corporate Planning Manager, Yorkshire Electricity Group

'Changes the way you think. Practical and useful, from authors who really understand synergy.'

Bjarne Eriksen
Chief Executive, Skandinavisk

'The combination of innovative thinking, clear analysis, and practical advice makes *Synergy* an exceptional book. Campbell and Goold's insight will give real help to managers who want to (or need to) make collaboration add value to their business.'

Peter Smith
Chief Executive, The Norton Rose M5 Group

'Andrew Campbell and Michael Goold's work provides a fresh perspective on one of today's most critical managerial challenges, by rethinking the very nature of synergy.'

Dr Francesco de Leo
Director, Telecom Italia

'In the search for ways of maximising performance by tackling synergy issues, we have found Campbell and Goold's insightful framework both helpful and practical.'

Tim Stevenson
Chief Executive, Castrol International

'Practical, penetrating and effective. Will help clear your thinking about linkages.'

Tom Moloney
Chief Executive, EMAP Consumer Magazines UK

'Campbell and Goold tackle the difficult subject of synergy head on. They destroy old myths and provide new insights into how to realise synergistic opportunities. More importantly they explain why many attempts to create synergy fail. This book should be compulsory reading for all senior managers, particularly those in holding companies.'

Phillip Blackler
Chief Operating Officer, Fugro NV

Synergy

*Why links between business units often fail
and how to make them work*

Andrew Campbell

and

Michael Goold

CAPSTONE

The right of Andrew Campbell and Michael Goold to be identified as the authors of this work has been asserted in accordance with the Copyright, Designs and Patents Act 1988

First Published 1998 by
Capstone Publishing Limited
Oxford Centre for Innovation
Mill Street
Oxford OX2 0JX
United Kingdom

British Library Cataloguing in Publication Data
A CIP catalogue record for this book is available from the British Library

ISBN 1-900961-57-1

Typeset in 11/15 pt Bembo by
Sparks Computer Solutions, Oxford
http://www.sparks.co.uk
Printed and bound by
T.J. International Ltd, Padstow, Cornwall

This book is printed on acid-free paper

Contents

Executive Summary

Preface

Explains the intellectual development that lies behind this book and the history of ideas presented.

1   Why Is Synergy Difficult?

Synergy is difficult not just because of the wide range of possible solutions to choose from or because of the problems of cost/benefit analysis. Synergy is difficult because of four biases in most managers' minds – synergy bias, parenting presumption, skill presumption and neglect of downsides.

The antidotes to these biases are four mental disciplines – size the prize, pinpoint the parenting opportunity, build on parenting skills, look for downsides.

2   Size the Prize

It is not easy to estimate how big a synergy benefit will be. Three practical steps help managers size the benefits and reduce the impact of the synergy bias:

- disaggregate benefits to gain greater clarity and precision
- frame the initiative to help separate primary from secondary benefits and give focus for action
- size the prize by making order of magnitude financial and strategic judgements and noting opportunity costs and compromise costs.

3   Pinpoint the Parenting Opportunity

There is no reason for managers in the parent company to intervene unless something is stopping business unit managers from doing the commercially sensible thing. Parenting opportunities occur because business managers

- have not perceived the benefits
- have mis-evaluated the size of the benefits
- are not motivated to help create the benefits
- do not have the capabilities or mechanisms to create the benefits.

In each of these four areas of parenting opportunity there are different 'causes' of the opportunity and different 'roles' for parent managers to play. By pinpointing the opportunity, parent managers can clarify the role they need to play and identify possible interventions that would be beneficial.

4   Build on Parenting Skills

It requires skills to influence business unit managers to do something they are not choosing to do already. What is more, the parenting skills needed are different for different areas of synergy. Before choosing an intervention, parent managers need to judge whether they have or can build the skills to implement it.

In our experience the chances of success are low unless the company has either

- a well-grooved mechanism: an intervention that has been used successfully before to achieve similar kinds of synergy benefits; or

- a natural champion: an individual with the specialist knowledge, organisational respect, people skills, time and desire to make the intervention work.

Without a well-grooved mechanism or a natural champion, the chances of success are low.

5   Look for Downsides

Downsides and upsides can occur in four areas:

- *Business mindsets:* The commercial strategies and rules of thumb that managers use to run their businesses. Links between business units can improve or contaminate current mindsets.
- *Organisational dynamics:* The direction of change in the culture and way the organisation works. Linkage interventions can support or hinder the changes that are underway.
- *Other parenting influences:* The impact parent managers are trying to have in other areas such as performance management. Interventions can facilitate or disrupt the other influences the parent is trying to have.
- *Motivation/innovation:* The energy in the organisation and the commitment to creativity and invention. Links can reduce or enhance feelings of ownership, team working and competitiveness which are often critical to motivation and innovation.

Parent managers particularly need to look out for downsides because of the mental bias in favour of upside thinking.

6   Deciding What to Do

In situations where an intuitive decision is not sufficient, managers can use a more structured process for choosing interventions.

First, managers need to 'size the prize' and 'pinpoint the parenting opportunity'. When the prize is small or there is no parenting opportunity, no intervention is necessary. When the prize or the parenting opportunity is uncertain, an 'exploratory' intervention is called for.

If the prize is substantial and the parenting opportunity clear, managers then need to define three alternative interventions that address the parenting opportunity.

The final step is to evaluate these three interventions against three criteria – impact on the parenting opportunity, ease of implementation and knock-on effects. If all interventions have high implementation or downside risks, no action should be taken. Otherwise a choice is made by considering which intervention will give the best overall outcome.

7 Taking Stock: How Well Is Your Approach to Synergy Working?

Some companies will benefit from a general review of their approach to synergy. This involves:

- identifying the main areas of synergy potential and their likely impact on performance
- documenting the current approach to synergy, including its status in the overall corporate strategy
- judging the effectiveness of the current approach in releasing the synergies
- drawing up an agenda for change in organisation, strategy and mechanisms, including developing a list of links that need to be created.

Reviewing a company's overall approach is a major task and may not be worth the effort unless there are clear signals that change is needed.

Epilogue

Summarises the lessons that have been learnt from our ten years of research on synergy. Takes three perspectives: the parent manager, the business unit manager and the researcher.

Preface

Managers and academics are fascinated by synergy. It has become one of management's top priorities. It is a way of getting extra performance, creating new businesses, and making more profit from the existing situation. It is a logic that drives acquisitions and empire building. It is a glue that creates community out of disparate entities.

Yet synergy can be as elusive as the Holy Grail. Academics have described the theory of synergy, but have few practical examples. Managers make appeals for co-operation, but talk more about the not-invented–here syndrome. Recent books, such as *The Synergy Myth* and *The Synergy Trap*, argue against synergy, suggesting it is a mirage. In this book we want to take the first close-in look at how synergy happens, why it doesn't happen, and what managers can do about it.

The book has a long history. Its origins can be traced back to a conversation with Sigurd Reinton, then a Director of McKinsey & Co. Sigurd had studied a research report we wrote in 1985, entitled 'The Role of the Corporate Centre in Diversified Corporations'. He was highly supportive of the work we were doing, and in particular of the question we had been asking: 'How do corporate centres add value to the businesses they own?' (a question that had been injected into our thinking by Professor John Stopford, then head of the Centre for Business Strategy at the London Business School).

Sigurd's main criticism of our work was that it did not give enough attention to the horizontal links between business units in large companies. He claimed that we had researched the vertical relationship between the corporate centre and its businesses, but we had not examined the lateral relationships between sister companies. 'How do these relationships create value,' he asked, 'and what is the role of the corporate centre in creating co-ordination and linkages?'

Our discussions with McKinsey evolved into a joint research project. The project focused on the skills that corporate centres have that enable them to create value, and we gave special attention to the way the centre manages synergies and linkages. The project attempted to distinguish between companies that largely ignore cross business links, companies that seek synergies mainly from skill sharing, and companies that seek to combine some resources across business units in the form of common purchasing, research, manufacturing, branding, selling or distribution. But this classification didn't really work. We found that most companies do a bit of everything.

The trail then went dead as we focused on research in other areas – corporate mission and systems of strategic control. But in 1990 we returned to the issue of horizontal linkages, and launched a research project loosely titled 'Synergy and Linkages in Multibusiness Companies'. The fieldwork for this project involved documenting the synergy benefits being achieved in a sample of companies such as 3M, Mars, Shell and Unilever. We focused on linkage benefit stories. In these, a beneficiary (a manager in a business unit who was prepared to claim that he or she had received a benefit from some linkage with a sister company) told us how the benefit had come about. Our aim was to identify useful generalisations about how a corporation could stimulate beneficial linkages between business units.

Again we were frustrated. Our data bank of linkage benefit stories was certainly interesting – but its main value was in providing evidence that undermined most of the generalisations current at the time. For example, we found that, contrary to conventional wisdom, benefits could be achieved without dense networks or trust relationships. We found that co-operation often happens without any influence from the centre. Also, we found that successful companies have well defined ways of achieving benefits, but that these ways differ by function and even by issue. Finding workable generalisations about 'how to achieve linkage benefits' proved to be hard. In the face of these findings, we narrowed our research down to one type of linkage – skill sharing – and developed some ideas about how corporate centre managers should approach the issues of building and sharing skills across units. (*Core Competency-Based Strategy*, Andrew Campbell and Kathleen Sommers Luchs, International Thomson Publishing 1997.)

Meanwhile, we were devoting the bulk of our attention to the larger debate about corporate strategy. Against a background of 'conglomerate discounts' and increasing market sentiment in favour of 'focus', we started a research project to determine the ingredients of successful corporate-level strategies. We wanted to understand why some companies successfully build value through a strategy of diversification while others do not. The synergy issue was an important component of this work. We recognised that a number of successful diversified companies such as Emerson or Rio Tinto put little effort into managing links between units, while others such as Canon and Unilever talk of little else.

The breakthrough which led to this book came from our Ashridge colleague, Marcus Alexander. Marcus was researching companies such as ABB, American Express and Canon that claimed linkage or synergy management as a central strand of their corporate strategy. Why, he wondered, were ABB's and Canon's efforts successful while those of American Express had mixed results at best? What light could be thrown on the issues by the synergy success stories in our database?

As he pondered these questions, Marcus came to the conclusion that most companies were looking at the synergy issue the wrong way round. The normal assumption was that it was part of the corporate centre's job to be actively looking for and developing lateral links between the businesses in its portfolio. What's more, companies should only consider diversification where those kinds of links could be identified and pushed through. Yet at the same time, managers (and academics) were noting that many, if not most, of these planned synergies failed to materialise. Moreover, most managers' gut feelings were that synergy is a tricky topic, more often the pretext for interfering corporate managers to push for inappropriate links than the source of real and lasting performance improvements.

The managers' gut feel wasn't wrong. Marcus provided the intellectual rationale for their scepticism by standing the accepted theory on its
head. *It only makes sense to use synergy as a logic for diversification if there is
something blocking independent companies from working together in joint ventures, alliances or trading relationships.* Unless there is a blockage that is
interfering with the natural market mechanisms, there is no reason to
suppose that the links will be better managed within a larger parent
organisation than between profit-seeking independent companies.
Marcus's blockage theory explained the failures and, at the same time,
provided a framework for understanding the rare examples of success.

Efforts to manage linkages, we realised, would only be likely to work
when both of two conditions applied: when blockages were interfering
with normal commercial behaviour and the corporate centre managers
had resources or skills that would enable them to remove or overcome
the blockages. Failures are caused by the absence of one or other of
these circumstances. The scarcity of success is due to the rarity of both
conditions coinciding.

The project on corporate-level strategy was completed in 1994 and,
once it had been published (*Corporate-Level Strategy: Creating Value in the
Multibusiness Company*, Michael Goold, Andrew Campbell and Marcus
Alexander, John Wiley & Sons 1994), we were keen to return to the
topic of synergy to see if the blockages concept would help us develop
our thinking further. The Research Committee of the Ashridge Strategic
Management Centre, made up of representatives of the companies that
support our research, was in no doubt that we should focus the work on
developing practical guidance rather than new theory. The corporate
members of the Research Committee wanted help with linkage decisions.

We now had a framework and a focus. The new project was entitled
'A Practical Approach to Synergy'. Fieldwork involved identifying managers with synergy issues, finding out how they were thinking about the
decisions they faced, testing whether our ideas were of any practical use
to them, and writing up case studies from which to generalise. This book
is the result.

Its novelty, we believe, is precisely that it is written as a practical guide.
We know that synergy initiatives can yield huge benefits and that linkages

play a vital role in some companies' strategies. But we also recognise that managers find decision making about linkages difficult. We therefore recommend some ways of thinking and some mental disciplines which help managers to cut through the biases and frustrations that so often derail synergy efforts. By following these disciplines, which are firmly grounded in Marcus Alexander's blockage theory – described in Chapter 3 under the label of 'parenting opportunities' - it is much easier to zero in on those synergy initiatives that have real potential and steer clear of dead ends that waste everybody's time and energy.

To make the book as useful as possible, we have included numerous examples and anecdotes. With a few exceptions, we have not named the companies or the people involved. There is a good reason for this. For a notoriously tricky subject like synergy, it was particularly important to be able to describe failures as well as successes, and to be able to be open about the frustrations and pitfalls managers so frequently face when trying to create linkages. For this reason, we have disguised many of our examples, or at least made them anonymous. We needed to be able to share real situations, acknowledge real human frailties and discuss real costs and benefits. We could only do this by going to some lengths to disguise our examples. What we hope is that readers may well react to our examples by saying: 'That's interesting. That seems just like a situation that occurred in our company.'

1
Why Is Synergy Difficult?

Synergy is difficult not just because of the wide range of possible solutions to choose from or because of the problems of cost/benefit analysis. Synergy is difficult because of four biases in most managers' minds – synergy bias, parenting presumption, skill presumption and neglect of downsides.

The antidotes to these biases are four mental disciplines – size the prize, pinpoint the parenting opportunity, build on parenting skills, look for downsides.

No question: managers find it hard to create synergy from the business units under their command. Our research findings are clear. Precious few are the managers who have responded to us with: 'Ah yes. Co-ordinating business units. Let me tell you how we do this. It's pretty straight forward. We ...'

Of course, some managers express strong enthusiasm for co-ordination and synergy. For example, executives at 3M, Canon, Mars, and Shell explain that certain kinds of linkages are vitally important and work well in their companies. From these success stories we have identified six different kinds of synergy – shared know-how, shared tangible resources, pooled negotiating power, co-ordinated strategies, vertical integration and combined new business development (see sidebar – 'Six types of synergy'). When these work well, benefits come in the form of lower costs, reduced duplication, more customer loyalty, higher prices, new products and services, and new business opportunities.

In the majority of companies, however, synergy initiatives lead to problems. Inappropriate compromises, higher operating costs, customer confusion, organisational complexity, reduced motivation and managers distracted from more important tasks are all common complaints. In these companies, corporate centre managers talk about co-ordination between business units with furrowed brows and stories of woe.

● A multi-business retailer was determined to develop some core competencies across a portfolio of similar businesses. The CEO identified three areas where he thought commonalities and co-ordination might be beneficial – supply chain management, marketing, and customer service. He launched three project teams to decide what to do. Each project team was chaired by a business-level chief executive to ensure grass roots support for the initiatives. Each project team also had support from well-respected consultants who knew the company.

All three projects struggled. Participants found it hard to agree on what was best practice, or what was the cause of good results in some areas. They resisted pooling their interests even in areas like warehousing,

Six types of synergy

- *Shared know-how*. The benefits associated with the sharing of knowledge and competencies across the portfolio. It may involve sharing of best practice in certain business processes, or leveraging expertise in functional areas, or pooling knowledge about how to succeed in specific geographical regions. The know-how may be written up in manuals, policies and procedures, but very often it is less formally documented. In some cases, it is more a matter of sharing the way that skilled managers go about their work. The emphasis that many companies now give to leveraging core competencies and sharing best practices reflects the importance of this type of synergy.

- *Shared tangible resources*. The benefits from economies of scale and elimination of duplicated effort when physical assets and resources are shared – for example, when businesses use a common manufacturing facility research laboratory. Companies often justify acquisitions of related businesses by the synergies and cost reductions that are anticipated from the sharing of resources.

- *Pooled negotiating power*. The cost or quality benefits that can be gained from purchasing scale. It also covers the benefits from joint negotiation with other stakeholders such as customers, governments, universities, etc. A number of companies have identified surprisingly large benefits through common purchasing of inputs used by several of their businesses.

- *Co-ordinated strategies*. The benefits that arise from aligning the strategies of two or more businesses: for example, by reducing competition between units (e.g. by allocating markets) or co-ordinating reactions to shared competitors (e.g. multi-point competition). In principle, this can be an important source of synergy benefits, but striking the right balance between corporate intervention and business unit autonomy is not easy.

- *Vertical integration*. Co-ordinating the flow of products or services from one unit to another. Benefits come from lower inventory costs, shared product development, better capacity utilisation and improved market access. In industries such as petrochemicals and forest products, well-managed vertical integration can yield major benefits.

- *Combined new business creation.* The creation of new businesses by combining know-how from different units, by extracting activities from different units to put into a new unit, and by internal joint ventures or alliances between units. With the increased concern for corporate regeneration and growth, several companies have placed added emphasis on this type of synergy.

where cost savings looked certain. They were reluctant to support the projects at all, arguing that they had better things to do with their time than 'search for hard to identify (and probably non-existent) synergies'. Within 12 months all three projects had been abandoned and another attempted linkage had failed.

● In another example, two business units of a large consulting company, one specialising in systems (IT) and the other in strategy, attempted to co-ordinate their efforts to develop a joint market for energy clients. By pooling their knowledge, the two business units were able to present an impressive proposition to some large energy companies. However, the co-ordination fell apart when it came to execution. A partner explained: 'We refer to it as the pizza problem. We had managers and staff from the two units working together on the assignment. One evening when they were working late, the strategy consultants suggested that they order in some pizza and charge it to the assignment. The IT consultants explained that they weren't allowed to do this: their terms of employment did not allow them to charge these sorts of items to client accounts. The conversation then turned to terms and conditions more generally, and soon the IT consultants discovered that the strategy consultants were being paid as much as 50% more and had better fringe benefits. Yet they were working together doing similar kinds of daily tasks.'

As the tension grew, it was decided to move the energy-related IT unit out of the systems business and into the strategy-consulting business. This would eliminate the friction and ease some other co-ordination difficulties. However, once the IT consultants were part of the strategy-consulting unit, they were exposed to the rigorous up-or-out evaluation policies common in strategy firms. Over time, all the IT consultants were pushed out of the firm, and five years after the initiative, not only was there little penetration of the energy market, not only had a number of good IT consultants been lost, but some deep bad feeling had built up between the two businesses.

These bad news anecdotes are surprisingly common. They are sometimes told to illustrate the complexity of the issues. But more often they are told to release heartfelt frustrations that something so simple as getting two members of the same family to work together could be so hard. A common response is one of exasperation at the behaviour of business-unit managers. 'How could they be so bone-headed, so perverse, so intransigent?' complained one manager. Another common response is weariness. 'One thing I have learnt is that you don't try to push co-ordination in this organisation. I have got my fingers burnt too many times,' bemoaned another.

A close in look at company behaviour reveals that the picture is not as black and white as these high-level stories suggest. Even 3M and Canon find some types of synergy hard to address; and even the most frustrated companies have some areas where links are working well. Yet the over-riding evidence is that synergy initiatives result in an unusually high level of frustration and disappointment. Why? What is so difficult about creating synergy between business units in the same portfolio?

Tough decisions to make

Our first thought was that synergy decisions might be in some way harder to make than other decisions. There are two aspects of these decisions that could account for this: the range of intervention choices available, and the difficulty of cost/benefit analysis.

First, there is a huge range of different types of interventions and mechanisms to choose from. Take, for example, the pursuit of core competencies by the multi-business retail company. The array of possible interventions that the CEO could have made is large. Instead of the project-team approach he adopted, he could have:

- asked all units to carry out benchmarking exercises in the chosen areas, including benchmarking with 'sister units';
- set demanding performance targets in the chosen areas and encouraged the units to talk to each other about possible ways of achieving the goals;
- encouraged networking between the managers in the chosen areas;
- designed cross unit career paths for managers in the chosen areas;
- created company-wide training programmes, conferences or forums for exchange in the chosen areas;
- hired an external consultant to analyse and recommend how co-ordination should be carried out;
- changed managers he thought were resisting;
- chosen more senior or more junior leaders for the project teams: he could even have chaired them himself;
- appointed corporate centre functional experts in these areas with small or large budgets and with limited or substantial powers;
- set corporate-wide policies of best practice;
- centralised areas like supply chain management.

Against this long list of options (and it could be still longer), it is not clear that the CEO made the right choice. Maybe such decisions are hard because there are too many options. Maybe frustration arises because it is too hard to evaluate all the choices.

Undoubtedly the range of choices makes the decision tough, and managers can benefit from practical guidance on how to choose between alternatives. But we do not believe that the wide range of choices is the main cause of frustration. In fact, the range of choices may be no wider for decisions about synergies than for other categories of management decision. It is certainly no wider than for decisions about what new product to launch or which manager to appoint to a particular position. If we are to understand the underlying reasons for frustration we must look somewhere else.

The second factor that might make linkage decisions especially difficult is the problem of cost/benefit analysis. It is true that in most such decisions both costs and benefits are hard to judge. The chief executive of the multi-business retail company was not certain that big benefits could be created from co-ordinating supply chain management, marketing or customer service. He felt confident that there would be benefits, but he had no way of proving his case to managers who believed the contrary.

Costs are often easier to assess than benefits because they are determined by the initiative that is taken. Yet even costs can be hard to estimate. How much management time will it take to make this joint effort work? It is likely to involve time from all the businesses concerned and from the corporate centre; but how much? Moreover, what is the cost of this management time? If it involves hard-pressed managers, it should be costed based on the value of the opportunity lost by choosing to focus on this task rather than some other priority. Without a detailed assessment of priorities, it can be hard to judge the costs. Maybe synergy decisions are frustrating because cost/benefit analysis is hard to pin down, making it easy for managers to disagree.

Exhibit 1.1   Four mental biases.

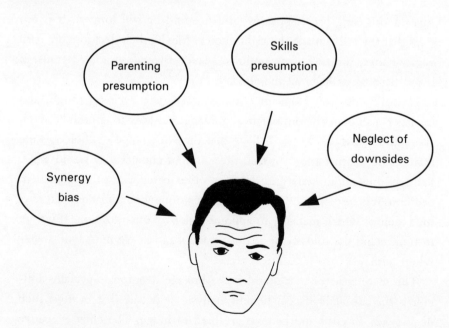

Certainly the difficulties of cost/benefit analysis make linkage decisions tough, particularly because co-ordination often requires agreement and commitment from managers in different areas with different views. But, again, we do not believe that this is the main cause of frustration. Cost/benefit analysis is tough for most managerial decisions.

The problem managers have with decisions about synergy may be partly to do with the wide range of options and partly to do with the difficulties of cost benefit analysis. But there must be other causes as well. Our research has identified four mental biases which we believe are the root cause of managers' frustrations in this area. These mental biases distort decision-making and cause a higher failure rate than in other areas of management (Exhibit 1.1).

Synergy bias

The first mental bias is the result of over-enthusiasm for synergy by parent managers. This is crucial because we believe that the quality of the interventions made by parent managers is the major determinant of successful linkages.

Throughout this book we will use the term 'parent managers' to distinguish managers who are part of the 'parent organisation' from 'business managers' who are part of business units (see sidebar, 'Corporate parenting'). A 'parent manager' can work at division, country or business-group level, not just at headquarters. From the perspective of parent managers, at whatever level, synergies are about getting business managers to work together in ways that create additional value.

It is synergy bias in the minds of parent managers that makes them see 'mirages': situations where they think they can see a valuable linkage opportunity when, in reality, it does not exist. It is not that linkage opportunities, like oases in the Sahara, are rare and hard to find. Rather, parent managers are like desert travellers eager for water. Thirsty and travelling in hope that the next rise will bring them in sight of their objective, they see synergies that aren't there.

Corporate parenting

Multi-business companies consist of a number of individual business units, which report to one or more levels of management above the business units. In addition to the corporate headquarters, these upper levels of management may include 'divisional', 'regional', 'group' or 'sector' management teams, together with their staff functions and support services. We refer to the levels of management above the business units as the corporate parent organisation. Exhibit 1.2 is a simplified organisation chart for a typical multi-business company.

Exhibit 1.2   A typical multi-business company.

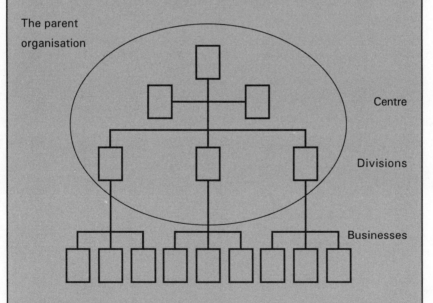

The business units are the market- or product-focused organisational entities that create value by serving external customers more cost-effectively than their competitors. They are normally run by a management team that is responsible for the profitability and performance of the unit.

The parent organisation has no external customers and generates no revenues of its own. Instead, its primary role is to influence the business units in ways that will cause them to perform better than they would if they were each independent companies. The aggregate performance of the multi-business corporate entity should be superior to what could be achieved by breaking the company up into a series of separate, independent businesses.

The promotion of linkages and synergies between the businesses, which is the focus of this book, is one of the ways in which the corporate parent can bring about better performance. If the parent helps to create beneficial linkages that would not have occurred without its influence, it can clearly claim to have enhanced performance.

Other ways in which parent managers can create better performance include:

- *stand-alone influence:* the guidance by parent managers of decisions that do not concern linkages with other units, but do affect the performance of each business as a stand-alone entity. Influence on setting a business's strategy, defining its targets, appointing its senior managers or approving its major investments are all important examples of stand-alone influence.
- *functional guidance:* the policies and expert advice that central functions can provide to business units with less expert functional skills
- *corporate development:* the buying, selling, venturing and redefining of business units.

The role of the corporate parent is described much more fully in *Corporate-Level Strategy: Creating Value in the Multibusiness Company* by Michael Goold, Andrew Campbell and Marcus Alexander (John Wiley & Sons, 1994).

Their thirst is driven by a belief that the main value-creating role of a parent manager is to promote synergy. 'If I am going to make this portfolio worth more than the sum of the parts, I need to drive some co-ordination benefits', is a frequently expressed view. 'We are a big group with many diverse interests. There must be areas where we could work together to help each other,' is another common view. Whether the logic is about making two plus two add up to more than four or making sure opportunities to work together are not overlooked, the result is the same. The parent manager feels a responsibility to find linkage opportunities and do something about them.

This self-imposed responsibility is harmful in two directions. It causes managers to chase nebulous synergies and overestimate their benefits. At the same time, it also causes them to overlook or underestimate the costs, particularly opportunity costs, of achieving these benefits. The result is a mirage: a synergy which looks enticing to parent managers, but which actually exists only in their minds.

This bias in favour of linkages is reinforced by wide use of the word 'synergy', and the current pressure on multi-business companies to provide a compelling reason for their existence. Most parent companies are looking for ways of justifying their current portfolio. Demergers, spinoffs, MBOs, breakups, decluttering, unbundling and other marketplace trends are causing parent organisations to question their mix of businesses.

In the 1970s and early 1980s it was acceptable to argue that the parent organisation was a holding company providing funds to the businesses and balancing the portfolio to create steady earnings performance. Now such an answer is not acceptable. Shareholders and commentators require each company to have a meaningful focus; and most parent managers are using the umbrella term 'synergy' to argue that their company is appropriately focused. As a result, there is a desperate search for the evidence that such a thing exists.

This high-stakes quest is often actively encouraged by a synergy bias on the part of business managers, too. It's natural to want to feel part of something bigger and to make sense of the larger organisation to which they belong. It's comforting – there's safety in numbers. And if they could just create the glue to hold it all together, they would be able to turn a loose commercial federation into a tight-knit clan.

This thirst for synergy creates optical illusions. Parent managers, often supported by business managers, believe that synergy already exists and that further initiatives will reveal more synergy benefits that up till now have been hidden from view. If parent managers *want* to believe that synergy opportunities exist, it is comparatively easy to make a case in favour – especially given the problems of precise cost/benefit analysis.

● In one famous example, Britain's largest industrial company, ICI, whose businesses ranged from chemicals to pharmaceuticals and from explosives to paints, used the synergy argument to fight off the hostile attentions of Hanson, Britain's most aggressive corporate raider. ICI argued that there were important technical linkages between its businesses that Hanson would not understand.

A year after ICI had successfully won this war of words and Hanson had withdrawn, ICI announced a demerger. The synergy between ICI's biosciences businesses and its commodity chemical businesses had not just evaporated, it had become a 'fault line'. Not only were the benefits of co-ordination argued to be insignificant, there were actually big disadvantages in staying together. And so, in fact, it proved, with the performance of the separate businesses far exceeding the performance of the two sets of businesses together.

The ICI example points to a common focus of synergy bias – co-ordinated research. Other targets of synergy bias include internal benchmarking, intertrading and central services. Parent managers often encourage their businesses to benchmark performance with each other, going to considerable expense to provide data that can help with comparisons. In our experience, the cost is only justified when the businesses are carrying out identical activities in different locations. If not, internal benchmarking is a mirage. The business units would be better off comparing themselves with a competitor or an independent company with similar operations.

● The chief executive of the multi-business retailer, seeking to develop core competencies across the group in supply chain management, marketing and customer service, may also have been chasing a mirage. Since his retail businesses were competing in different ways and offering different levels of service to their customers, internal benchmarking and common skill development were probably inappropriate.

Intertrading, another favourite of synergy seekers, also often turns out to be a mirage.

● A company with a road-building business also owned a quarrying operation. The chief executive was frustrated to note that only 30% of his
road-building contracts were being supplied from his quarries. After raising this point with his managers to little effect, he hired a consultant to
check out the situation. In a report costing £250,000, the consultant
told him that intertrading between the two businesses was a mirage.
Road-building contracts need to use stone from the quarry nearest to the
road project. Transport costs are sufficiently high that it does not make
sense to go further afield. The company's quarries were the nearest in
just 30% of the cases, suggesting that no intertrading opportunities were
being missed.

Added value from central services is another common illusion. What
happens is that parent managers spot similar activities being carried out
in a number of business units. Why not centralise these activities – market research, payroll, invoicing, distribution, production planning, security,
management training, etc. – and cut out duplication? Centralisation should
give economies of scale and allow for the recruitment of better quality
people to lead the service.

Unfortunately, the apparent opportunity frequently turns out to be a
mirage. The benefits are not as great as expected or the differences in
service levels needed by the businesses prove hard to deliver from one
unit. In fact, in those areas where the economies of scale or the benefits
of focused expertise are large, outside suppliers can often do a better job
than a central service.

To sum up: mirages are the result of a bias in the thinking and attitudes of parent managers. The bias exists because of the current focus on
synergy and the pressure to justify the existence of the portfolio of businesses. It is reinforced by the natural desire of parent managers to justify
their own jobs. If you appoint a corporate marketing, IT or manufacturing director, it is part of his or her job to hunt out opportunities for
co-ordination. Once you are aware of the synergy bias, it will be no
surprise that a proportion of them turn out to be mirages. Synergy bias
can also exist in the minds of business managers eager to feel part of
something larger than their business.

Parenting presumption

A second important bias stems from a false assumption made by many parent managers. They presume that an opportunity to gain synergies will not be addressed without their help. They presume that the business unit managers will not work together unless pushed. They presume that they need to 'parent' linkages.

This presumption has a number of causes. The first is a manager's natural belief that things need managing. In a controlled business-school experiment, individuals were told that they were managers of an advertising assistant who was developing a marketing concept for a new product and asked to evaluate the quality of the work. The participants were first shown a draft of the assistant's output and then the final story-board. Some participants were permitted to give advice on the draft in their capacity as managers, others were not. All participants were given the same final story-board to evaluate. The participants who felt (erroneously) that they had had a managerial input rated the final story board as being significantly better than those who did not.

The researcher tested the robustness of this result by repeating the experiment with a different set-up. The participants were told that they were colleagues of the advertising assistant rather than the assistant's manager. This time the participants who offered advice rated the final output exactly the same as those who did not. This confirmed that it was belief in the value of managerial advice, rather than peer advice, that caused the participants in the first experiments to give the final output a higher rating.

The second cause of the parenting presumption is a belief that business–unit managers suffer from a not-invented-here (NIH) attitude. Since business–unit managers frequently do resist initiatives from the parent company, parent managers have plenty of reinforcement for this belief. They presume that resistance stems from a blinkered mindset, and that attempts to get business managers to take a wider view are falling foul of it.

The belief in NIH reinforces the belief that linkages need to be parented and vice versa. Together they cause parent managers to have a bias towards intervening. They presume that synergy is not the natural state and will only come about if they intervene to encourage it.

In practice this is a false assumption. Business managers frequently co-operate with other businesses to achieve their objectives. Unless the atmosphere of the parent company actively discourages co-operation, there is no reason, a priori, to suppose that linkages need parenting. On the contrary: a more reasonable starting assumption is that business managers will normally find and execute linkages with other businesses that are appropriate – i.e. that NIH is not a factor unless proven otherwise. If the business-unit managers are not co-operating, there is probably a good reason.

Not only is the parenting presumption false, but a parenting presence may be part of the problem. In a classroom exercise we used to run, we observed an interesting phenomenon. The exercise involved two business-unit heads negotiating over a transfer-pricing problem in front of their corporate boss. In cases where the boss was present throughout the negotiation, a result was difficult to achieve. Mostly, the boss was forced to take a decision over the head of one or other of the business units, creating demotivation and bad feeling.

In cases where the boss withdrew from the negotiations, explaining that it was up to the businesses to resolve the problem, they usually reached an amicable solution. And they reached it more quickly. In other words, the presence of the parent in a management role made things worse rather than better.

For anyone approaching the finding with a parenting presumption, this is a remarkable result. But, in reality, it aligns with normal human behaviour. Siblings usually fight more vigorously when the good opinion of their parents is at stake. When the stakes are lower, they find it easier to get along.

We are not suggesting that links between sister units are *always* more difficult than links between independent units. It depends. Sometimes the influence of parent managers helps create an environment where co-ordination thrives, and sometimes it makes co-ordination more difficult. The important point is that the parenting presumption is false. Interference by the parent manager is not always necessary or appropriate.

Skill presumption

The third bias comes from another false assumption frequently made by parent managers. When they identify a synergy opportunity that is not being addressed, they automatically assume they have the skills to correct the situation. Frequently they don't: they don't have the necessary operating knowledge; they don't have the necessary relationships with the people who matter; they don't have the time, patience or force of character to follow through with implementation; or they don't have the facilitative skills to bring about agreement.

Linkages appear to work best when they are led by someone who is a 'natural champion' of the issue. This means that the person who leads the co-ordination has the appropriate technical knowledge, relationships, time, enthusiasm and facilitation skills. Contrary to the parenting presumption, the champion does not have to be a parent manager. He or she can be one of the business-unit managers. But where the parent manager takes the lead, failures are frequently caused by a lack of skill.

● In one example, the co-ordination was about component manufacturing and capacity sharing in an office furniture company. The company had factories in five countries, each supplying its own marketplace with unique products and components. Parent managers believed that the group could cut costs by using common components.

   The project was led by a corporate-centre manager with the help of consultants. The project team concluded that savings were possible. The heads of the businesses, however, fought the recommendations to a standstill. The problem was not mainly about the analysis. The project team had done detailed work that the heads of the businesses could not find fault with. The problem was the parent manager leading the project. He was an accountant whose manufacturing experience was limited. The local manufacturing directors did not respect him and feared that he would come up with impractical solutions. Despite appearing to go along with the project, they told their business heads of their unhappiness and their unwillingness to support the recommendations. Caught in the middle, the business heads had little option but to back their manufacturing directors.

Three years later a similar project was launched by a parent manager with a different background. He had worked for a rival office furniture-company, where he had successfully rationalised seven European factories down to three. Quickly gaining the respect of the manufacturing directors, he achieved a major improvement in the cost base by co-ordinating manufacturing across the group.

As we will explain later in the book, the skills, resources and culture of the parent organisation all affect its ability to make certain kinds of synergy happen. Moreover, skill and culture changes are frequently hard to bring about, and the appropriate resources are not always available from the market place. A presumption that the parent has or can readily acquire the skills needed to implement a particular synergy leads to naïve interventions, failure and frustration.

Neglect of downsides

The fourth and last bias is the tendency of parent managers to neglect the negative knock-on effects of their co-ordination initiatives. Knock-on effects are costs and benefits that occur as indirect outcomes of links between businesses. For example, links can affect other aspects of the relationship between the parent and the businesses; they can reinforce or oppose the direction of organisational change under-way in the company; they can impact motivation and innovation; they can produce a flow of ideas between businesses that go far beyond the intended focus.

These knock-on effects are described fully in Chapter 5. Suffice it to say here, however, that while parent managers often think about the upside of knock-on effects, they rarely consider the downside. Parent managers often give extra impetus to a synergy initiative 'because it will be an example to the rest of the organisation and help move us to a more co-operative philosophy', 'because it will encourage teamwork and the motivation and excitement of being part of a larger whole', or 'because managers in business A will benefit from rubbing shoulders with managers in business B'. It is rare for parent managers to hold back an initiative 'because it will put extra burden on a specific parent manager and hence reduce his ability to have influence in another area', 'because it might reduce ownership and commitment at the business unit level', or 'because managers in business–unit A might contaminate the thinking of managers in business unit B'.

Yet the downside knock–on effects are real. They need to be given more attention than they habitually get.

● For example, a consulting firm decided to create account managers for major clients across its three businesses – operations consulting, financial-systems consulting, and executive search. The operations-consulting and executive-search businesses had been acquired by the systems-consulting business and had separate brands. The objective of the account-manager was to bring the brands together, cross-sell products from different businesses and make sure that the left hand of the firm knew what the right hand was doing.

After just over 12 months, not only was the account manager concept abandoned in an atmosphere of recrimination and bad feeling between the businesses – the managing partner who introduced it was not re-elected. Some of the problems were the result of the inability of the account managers to understand the services of all three businesses. Others were due to the fact that clients appeared to prefer dealing directly with each business. In other words, the synergies were probably a mirage. However, the lasting damage caused by the intervention was not the result of the failure of benefits to emerge, it was the result of knock-on effects.

The executive-search business strongly resisted the initiative, claiming the need to have independent and confidential relationships with clients. When it went ahead anyway, there was a major loss of motivation among some senior consultants. Two partners left to form a rival business, taking some good clients with them. Relations between the leaders of the search business and parent managers deteriorated, damaging a number of other initiatives. The relationship only began to improve when the managing partner failed to obtain re-election.

The operations-consulting business was more supportive of the initiative, but suffered in a different way. Influenced by the financial-systems consultants, the operations business began directing its marketing at senior rather than middle managers. Joint presentations were made to many clients, and some operations consultants began to harbour ambitions to do more senior management consulting. The result: an increase in marketing costs and a slight reduction in total revenues, netting out as a significant reduction in profitability. It took some changes in the leadership of the operations business and a 'back-to-basics' strategy initiative to recapture its previous market position and profitability.

To be sure, this is a fairly extreme example. Not only were the anticipated synergies a mirage, the attempt to achieve them had some major negative effects. The important thing about the example is that the downsides were not even considered. When the firm's leaders set up the account-management system, they could see potential upsides, such as 'bringing the firm closer together', 'ensuring that more of our partners know what the other businesses do', and 'sharing ideas and best practice between businesses'.

Unfortunately they had not considered in any depth the potential downside effects. Managers who overlook the possibility of downsides are prone to interventions that are ill-judged or damaging.

Biases and frustrations

Because of the emphasis we place in this book on mirages and downsides, we are sometimes accused of being anti-synergy. 'If I worried about all the things you want me to worry about, I would never do anything', protested one manager. 'You are just against linkages', claimed another. We recognise why we are attacked in this way. Our approach to thinking about linkages is fundamentally more sceptical than the average parent manager.

On the other hand, we firmly believe that a more questioning stance will help most companies improve their linkage management. We happily acknowledge good synergy management can create large amounts of value – our work with companies like 3M, Canon, Mars and Unilever has demonstrated the size of the opportunity that exists in some portfolios. But we also know that such good management is rare. Much more common is the destruction of value by misguided attempts to create synergy: initiatives driven more by the four mental biases than by a balanced assessment of the potential for value creation.

● Highly public failures include American Express's much-written-up 'one enterprise' campaign designed to create synergy out of a spread of financial-services businesses, including the concept of a 'one-stop shop'. As with many other financial services companies, the attempt largely failed. James Robinson III, the architect of the campaign, was ousted, and the portfolio of businesses he had accumulated disbanded. Shearson Lehman, the brokerage and investment-banking combine, was disposed of at a loss to American Express of around $1 billion.

● Another large failure was the attempt by AT&T to integrate the computer manufacturer NCR with its telephone and equipment businesses. The result: value destruction estimated at over $4 billion by one academic, and the three-way break-up of the firm.

● Similar failures have been experienced by Japanese electronics firms seeking synergy from owning Hollywood studios, aerospace companies looking for value in combining with the automobile industry, and oil companies searching for commonalities with other extractive industries, such as minerals. There are plenty of well publicised problems and comparatively few well documented major successes.

We too are disappointed with the high incidence of failure and frustration in synergy management. That is why we have spent so long trying to understand the issues, and why we have written this book. Its purpose is precisely to remedy the situation by calling attention to the biases which we believe are the cause of the frustration and thus to help managers make better practical decisions about synergy. Since our case is that it is the quality of interventions by parent managers which is crucial in making synergies work or fail, it is to them that this book is primarily addressed. Much of what we say, of course, will be equally useful to business-unit managers seeking to understand the potential, but we do not explicitly address the problems and dilemmas they face.

In turn, our emphasis on parent managers has determined our choice of 'intervention' as the central, practical focus of the book. Why 'intervention'? Because, counter to conventional assumptions, we want to underline the nature of the act as an interference in the natural order of things. Granted, for many parent managers the word intervention is uncomfortable: too bossy, too interfering to describe some actions they take to promote cross-company collaboration. They would prefer to use terms like 'stimulate' or 'orchestrate' or 'set the context'.

While accepting this concern, we are not inclined to apologise. Our term is chosen to remind parent managers that they are altering normal behaviour. Whether the initiative involves changing incentives to encourage focus on corporate-wide results, organising management training to help build networks of relationships, designing information systems to foster freer flows of data, or simply encouraging managers to influence each other – the action has consequences which need to be thought through. Just as important, we want managers to think about what would happen if they *didn't* intervene – and why. What difference is their intervening designed to achieve? We want to emphasise that there is a choice. Not to intervene, in our terms, is very far from an admission of failure. In many cases it is the right and rational decision.

As we have observed, there are many different ways of intervening. At one extreme are drastic measures such as changing managers or issuing instructions. At the other extreme are subtle interventions such as bringing people together or gradually changing attitudes. The mere presence of a parent manager is a form of intervention. Interventions may require considerable amounts of the parent's time in monitoring, reinforcing, arbitrating and energising. Alternatively they may require no time at all. Interventions may involve centralising, controlling and building central staffs, or they may involve decentralising, empowering and delayering. We are keen to help parent managers make informed choices between all of these alternatives.

Practical guidance

Our practical guidance comes in two parts. The first part consists of 'mental disciplines' that will help parent managers avoid the four synergy biases. We have tried to make these mental disciplines as practical as possible by giving rules of thumb and guiding thoughts. They are, however, mainly about ways of thinking that act as antidotes to the biases. In consequence, managers will need to spend time on each discipline to get attuned. The second part of our practical advice is a decision framework that helps managers make tough choices. The framework is a way of structuring the decision process and is primarily designed for important and complex decisions, where the right way forward is uncertain or contentious.

The four mental disciplines (Exhibit 1.3) are about ways of thinking. Most people do not analyse situations in an ordered or organised way. They do not have time, and the issues do not present themselves in ways that make ordered analysis easy. Most people identify problems and light upon possible solutions all in the same thought. The human mind has great powers of synthesis and of intuitive judgement. Most managers

Exhibit 1.3 Four mental disciplines.

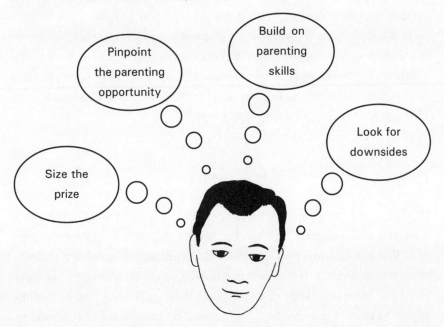

juggle options against facts in a holistic way, considering new options and new facts as they occur, calling for more analysis or more creative thinking only if the current conclusions do not 'feel' right. Rather than provide a step-by-step analytical process, we believe it is more helpful to identify mental disciplines that managers can use to keep their thinking straight.

The four mental disciplines (described in Chapters 2–5) are as follows.

Size the prize

Frequently, parent managers think about benefits in vague terms such as 'best-practice sharing' or 'co-ordinating relationships with customers'. This level of aggregation just makes the 'synergy bias' more likely. Who would argue that there are no opportunities to share best practice or no need to explore customer co-ordination?

By trying to be more precise, by developing a clear definition of the targeted benefit and where possible sizing the benefit, managers can counteract the synergy bias: defining the benefit as precisely as possible is a mental discipline that helps keep the synergy bias at bay.

It is also helpful in other ways. A precise definition of the objective can help point to appropriate interventions. Sizing the benefit can help avoid unimportant issues and provide a priority ranking for important issues. A clear benefit definition also helps with the next mental discipline: pinpoint the parenting opportunity.

Pinpoint the parenting opportunity

If it is possible to define a clear benefit, we would expect business–unit managers to co-operate in whatever way is necessary to release the benefit. We would not expect profit-seeking managers wantonly to leave money on the table. If they are not linking to release a benefit, we need to know why: this will tell us whether there is an opportunity for the parent to correct the situation. By focusing on the parenting opportunity, by asking why business managers are not co-operating, parent managers can confront the 'parenting presumption'. Rather than presume that the business managers need help to co-ordinate, this mental discipline encourages the opposite: business managers are presumed only to need the parent's assistance if there is something stopping them from doing what makes commercial good sense. An analysis of parenting opportunities is therefore an antidote to the parenting presumption.

By understanding parenting opportunities, we can also help to expose mirages. It is another way of resisting the synergy bias. Frequently, the reason why business managers are not co-ordinating is because they see large opportunity costs: they have other pressing priorities or they may be able to see more clearly the amount of time a linkage will absorb. If the views of business managers are right, if the opportunity costs are large or the commitment has been underestimated, then the linkage initiative may not offer a net benefit at all. It may be a mirage. A focus on parenting opportunities is therefore a doubly useful mental discipline.

Build on parenting skills

Linkage initiatives often fail because parent managers do not have the skills to implement the intervention they have chosen. We therefore recommend that parent managers explicitly list the skills needed to make an intervention work and equally explicitly decide whether they have or can acquire these skills. Put another way, parent managers need to assess how difficult and how risky implementation will be.

By focusing on the parenting skills needed and comparing them with those available, managers can resist the 'skills presumption'. Some interventions will be 'well grooved', requiring no new skills to implement. Others, however, will involve unfamiliar actions requiring new skills. By defining these skills as precisely as possible, parent managers can make a reasoned assessment of how easy implementation will be, and can choose interventions that build on available skills. This discipline encourages them to avoid hard-to-implement interventions and reduces the tendency to assume that they have the skills needed to make the synergy work.

Look for downsides

Linkage interventions normally have an impact wider than that directly intended. We propose that parent managers consider the potential knock-on effects explicitly. For some interventions, knock-on effects are small and can be ignored. But most interventions will have a complex mix of positive and negative knock-on effects.

By giving conscious consideration to these effects, by listing the expected impact and risks, managers can avoid neglecting downsides. We do not propose that managers focus exclusively on downsides, since this could lead to its opposite, neglect of upsides. Instead, we propose a broad assessment of possible indirect consequences that ensures downsides are considered along with upsides.

These four disciplines are not an ordered check-list of things to do, nor do they form a linear process of analysis. They are ways of thinking; ways of preventing the mind from being misled by synergy bias, parenting presumption, skill presumption and insufficient attention to downsides. Once the principles behind the disciplines have been absorbed, the mind has taken the medicine and should be less susceptible to the causes of frustration.

The mental disciplines help managers to get their thinking straight. They do not take the decision. To provide some help with the final choice: what intervention or bundle of interventions to make – we therefore also offer a framework that incorporates the mental disciplines in a structured sequence of thinking.

Decision framework

The decision framework, described in Chapter 6, is diagrammed in Exhibit 1.4. The circles in Exhibit 1.4 are the four mental disciplines. The square boxes provide the additional structuring needed to harness these disciplines into a decision process. Start, we suggest, with sizing the prize, followed by pinpointing the parenting opportunity. If the benefit is small,

Exhibit 1.4   Decision framework.

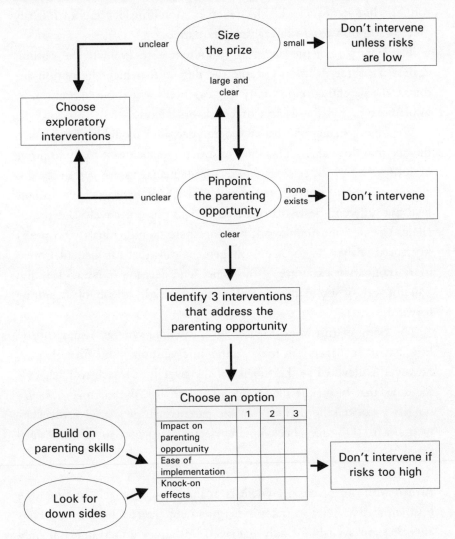

the intervention may be abandoned at that point. If there is no parenting opportunity, no further action is needed. If the benefit is unclear or the parenting opportunity hard to pin down, an exploratory intervention is called for that will resolve some of the uncertainties.

Once a substantial benefit has been defined and the parenting opportunity is understood, different options should be considered. This is normally a process of reducing a wide range of choices to a few front runners, but it can also be the reverse: stretching beyond an initially preferred option to create realistic alternatives.

The final part of the decision flow-chart is to evaluate the options against the three decision criteria: the degree to which the option addresses the parenting opportunity, the ease with which the option can be implemented, and the impact of knock-on effects.

We are not suggesting that all synergy decisions should be put through the decision flow-chart. This kind of structured analysis is likely to prove useful for complex decisions where parent managers are genuinely uncertain about what intervention to make, or where managers have strongly held but different views that need to be laid out objectively and reconciled. The decision framework provides help to individuals who prefer structured analysis or for tough judgement calls that can benefit from a more transparent exposure of the logic. The decision framework is also a useful way of summarising some of the principles this book is putting forward.

The body of this book focuses on individual synergy issues and on how parent managers can make better interventions. Our final chapter, however, is devoted to the subject of the overall approach to linkages – focusing, that is, on the macro-design rather than the micro-issues. We suggest a stocktaking that will enable parent managers to give their approach a 10,000-mile check-up and decide what individual issues need more attention.

★★★

Armed with our practical guidelines, managers will be able to avoid the frustrations that beset so many synergy attempts and mine the real benefits that are available. Badly managed initiatives undermine not only performance, but also the self-confidence that is so critical to organisation success. Well-managed efforts, on the other hand, create substantial value, and in some companies, are a vital plank in the corporate strategy. We believe this book will help managers address synergy issues with a new confidence: confident for the first time that they have a way of thinking and a framework for tackling tough decisions and confident that they will create fusion rather than frustration.

2
Size the Prize

It is not easy to estimate how big a synergy benefit will be. Three practical steps help managers size the benefits and reduce the impact of the synergy bias:

- disaggregate benefits to gain greater clarity and precision
- frame the initiative to help separate primary from secondary benefits and give focus for action
- size the prize by making order of magnitude financial and strategic judgements and noting opportunity costs and compromise costs.

The first of our disciplines for combating synergy biases underlines the importance of clearly defining the benefit. What exactly is the linkage initiative designed to achieve? Too often managers make synergy interventions with only a vague idea of the benefit that will ensue. Lack of clarity about the pay-off leads to a number of problems: interventions are poorly targeted; business managers are confused about what they are supposed to be doing; and, most important of all, parent managers find it hard to distinguish between real benefits and mirages.

● In a consumer goods company, management had recently created a central function to help co-ordinate product categories across geographically organised business units. There was a category for frozen vegetables and another for pasta, etc. Category managers were put 'in charge of' international brands and held responsible for creating 'leverage' across the business units. But as they began to develop mechanisms to help them with their responsibilities, the category managers found the vague definitions of the benefits they were pursuing – 'leverage' and 'developing international brands' – insufficient and confusing.

   For example, they were not sure what 'developing international brands' meant in practice. Did it mean working up a standard presentation of the brand so that it was recognisable to cross-border travellers and could be presented on multi-country media? Did it mean reducing duplication of marketing expenditure, so as to gain cost savings and eliminate bad practice? Or did it mean transferring knowledge of products and market segments between countries? Differences of opinion among category managers were matched by those among country-based product managers: different product managers were expecting different benefits from the new management structure.

   The lack of clarity made the category manager's job harder. A category manager visiting Argentina was trying to persuade the local product manager to launch a new food product using the marketing campaign that had been successful in other countries. The product manager was resisting. 'Thank you for the ideas, but I think we will need a different kind of marketing campaign in Argentina', he commented. 'I don't think you understand', responded the category manager, 'I am trying to create an international brand and this means standardizing the marketing between South America and Europe'.

Because it was not clear what being 'in charge of' international brands meant, it was also unclear how far the category managers should centralise decision making. If the main benefit of international brands was standardising brand presentation so that it could be recognised by cross-border travellers and advertised on multi-country media, then category managers would need to centralise decisions on positioning and presentation. If, on the other hand, the main potential benefit was reducing duplication of marketing effort and eliminating bad practice, rather than centralise decision-making, category managers would need authority to challenge plans and, where appropriate, veto proposals. Different definitions of the pay-off suggest different levels of centralisation and different types of intervention. Vague or excessively aggregated definitions of the benefit can produce mirages and misguided interventions.

● In one category, the category manager decided that the best intervention would be to appoint a lead country for each brand. The lead country was made responsible for managing the brand internationally. The lead countries chose to lay down tightly defined policies for the presentation and positioning of their brands, and refused to allow the use of the brand name in situations that did not meet the guidelines. As a result, the number of brands proliferated as non-lead countries opted to develop their own brands rather than live with the restrictions imposed by the lead country. A certain standardisation was achieved, but at the expense of internationalisation. Moreover, the lead countries paid little or no attention to the other potential sources of benefit, reducing duplication and avoiding the reinvention of bad practice, since they felt awkward overseeing the marketing efforts in other countries. If the category manager had defined the prize he was pursuing more carefully, he would probably have chosen different, and better, interventions.

There are three practical steps that are useful in getting a clearer definition of the benefit: disaggregation for greater precision, framing to separate primary from secondary benefits, and sizing the prize to ensure that a net benefit exists.

Disaggregation

The best way to clarify the nature of the benefit is to dig into the details. Rather than talk broadly of 'leverage across international brand positions', the category managers should have tried to determine what the different components of this broad benefit might be. They should have disaggregated the overall benefit into the more detailed constituent elements that lie behind it. Disaggregation allows much greater precision, about both the benefits that are and are not being sought.

Exhibit 2.1   Disaggregating the category management issue.

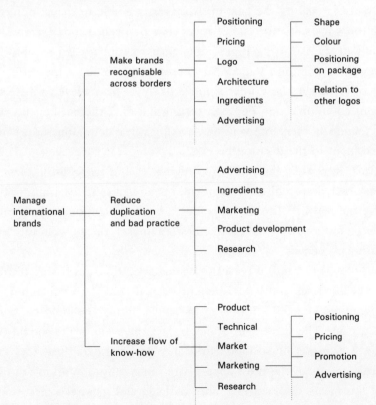

We have found that a sort of 'tree' form, in which the broad benefit area is decomposed into successively greater levels of detail, is a useful way to make the benefits explicit. Exhibit 2.1 shows how 'manage international brands' can be broken down into more and more detailed levels of component benefits. Thus the three main benefits at the first level of disaggregation are 'make brands recognisable across borders', 'reduce duplication and bad practice' and 'increase the flow of know-how'. These benefits can then be subdivided again. For example, the transfer-of-know-how benefit can be segmented into categories, such as product knowledge, technical support, market knowledge, marketing know-how, research know-how, etc. The brand-standardisation benefit can be broken down into different aspects of presentation, brand positioning, price, logo, product technology, etc. In other words, the management of international brands can be broken down into many different areas of possible benefit.

By disaggregating the benefit, managers are able to focus more precisely on what initiative or initiatives may be needed. For example, the benefit of standardising ingredients across countries is probably best achieved by common standards; whereas the benefit of increasing the flow of technical know-how is more likely to be achieved by creating lines of communication between technical staff. Different benefits typically require different interventions, making a clear definition of the benefit a vital input to the decision process.

If managers assess linkages at too high a level of aggregation, there is a danger that there will be disagreements and misunderstandings about where the real benefits are supposed to lie. Interventions will therefore either be too broad to achieve the desired impact, or not well directed at the primary benefit.

On the other hand, it is clear that disaggregation can be taken to the point where each individual benefit is small and the total number of disaggregated benefits is too large to handle. How far should the parent manager go? The answer, in principle, is simple. He or she should continue to disaggregate so long as the next level of detail provides extra information about the most appropriate intervention. Working through what this means in practice is more difficult, and requires a clear understanding of the businesses concerned.

For the category managers, the first level of disaggregation is certainly valuable. Not only does it help define what is meant by international brands, but it also suggests the sort of intervention that would be appropriate for different kinds of benefit: for example, communication forums would help to increase the flow of know-how, and central policies would help to standardise the brand. The next level of detail is also useful. By articulating the different types of know-how that can be transferred, category managers can consider how best to intervene for each type. They can also think about areas of overlap with other functions, such as research and manufacturing. Each of these functions will be seeking to foster sharing, and the areas of overlap will need to be defined and reviewed accordingly. The next level of detail – segmenting each type of know-how or presentation component into a series of sub-categories – is likely to be less useful, because it provides no new insights into the type of intervention needed. Choosing the appropriate level of disaggregation is an important art. As a rule of thumb, dig down at least one layer below the level at which the opportunity is initially formulated to see whether it yields additional insight.

● In some cases, the appropriate level of detail can be several layers down. One category manager was wrestling with an issue concerning packaging for a product that sold in most countries. He had disaggregated to a surprisingly rich level of detail, but felt finally that he was getting purchase on the decision. He had identified a large number of different packaging decisions – the type and colour of the cap, the type of material, the size, shape and colour of the bottle, the size and shape of the label, its positioning, and so on.

    As it turned out, each of these detailed decisions offered different benefits and required different interventions. For example, the type of cap was not only a big cost factor with major economies of scale because of the cost of moulds, it was also a major marketing issue. Different consumers preferred different caps. To create synergy, a project team was assembled to identify those countries that could share the same cap moulds and to test whether the extra costs incurred by other countries would really be justified by the marketing benefits.

The colour of the bottle involved different benefits and a different intervention. Changes in colour have little impact on manufacturing costs, so long as the shape is identical. Hence, colour standardisation was not an economic issue. It was, however, an issue in making the product into an internationally recognised brand. The appropriate intervention was to give authority for defining the colour choices to the international brand manager.

This example clearly illustrates the level of detail that is sometimes necessary to define the benefits with precision. Our advice is to continue to disaggregate so long as you are gaining extra insight and understanding. If an extra level of disaggregation is not yielding greater clarity on where the real benefits lie or on the nature of the initiative required, or if the extra precision is actually clouding the issue, pull back to the level at which you get the greatest purchase on the managerial action needed.

● A second example may further illustrate the importance of disaggregation. A company with three businesses, each offering different consulting and training services, shared a common brand and marketed these services to many of the same customers – human resource functions and senior managers.

Noting that each business had its own database of contacts, the group chief executive decided that there would be benefits in combining the databases. When he suggested setting up a central, common contact list, however, the units resisted strongly. He was only able to resolve the impasse by disaggregating the benefits and clarifying his objectives.

Exhibit 2.2 shows the different benefits that were identified. Some of the benefits were about ensuring that the mailing activity was having the right impact in the market place.

Others related to the sophistication and effectiveness of the direct mail activity. With a central resource, the chief executive felt he could afford better quality staff and equipment. Still other benefits related to cost reduction, combining mailings, eliminating duplicate names and reducing the total costs of managing the databases. Having disaggregated the benefits, the chief executive felt even more convinced that central control would be beneficial.

Exhibit 2.2   DIsaggregating the database issue.

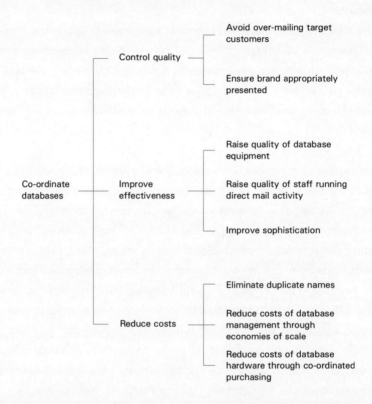

In reply, the businesses explained that nearly all the benefits could be achieved without centralising the databases. They could draw up policy statements to protect the brand. Annual mailing plans could identify customers who might be over-mailed. Quality of equipment and management could be improved by using consultants. And they could achieve most of the cost reductions by better co-ordination between the three businesses.

Behind the resistance were a number of factors. The businesses were reluctant to agree to centralisation because they were afraid of losing control over an important element of their success. They often changed mailing plans at short notice to reflect particular marketing needs, and they were anxious not to lose this flexibility. Moreover, the chief executive did not have a good track record with central service departments. Other centralising initiatives had run into trouble because the head of the central service had been insufficiently expert, too controlling or too bureaucratic.

By disaggregating the broader benefit ('co-ordinate databases'), the chief executive was able to think more clearly about his objectives and find a way of handling the impasse between the centre and the businesses. He decided that his objective of co-ordinating databases should be broken down into four different projects with different objectives (see page 41).

The examples we have discussed underline the value of having a precise definition of the benefits. Without this definition, it is easy to pursue a mirage, or set up an intervention that is only partly successful or even makes things worse. For example, the choice of lead countries as a way of getting the benefits of international brands turned out to be net negative in some cases. Germany was chosen as the lead country for a particular noodle product. The product also sold in significant quantities in France and the UK. Problems immediately arose between Germany and the other two major countries, France and the UK, where the product was differently positioned because of different eating habits. Moreover, the German use of the product was not the norm — most other countries fitted better with the French and UK positionings. Not surprisingly, attempts by the German product manager to impose standards for the brand met with stiff resistance and the subsequent disagreements clearly had net negative effects. The product manager spent much of his time in trying to resolve differences. A product re-launch in the UK was delayed by 18 months. A number of products were launched in other countries under locally created brands, with sub-optimal results. These countries felt the German brand policies were too restrictive. The net result was a slowing down of the internationalisation of the product concept and brand name.

With greater disaggregation, the category manager might have spotted that the imposition of inflexible brand standards would be inappropriate. Some sharing of the brand name might have been possible, so long as the standards were loosely defined in terms of product positioning and packaging. Some sharing of marketing campaigns might have been possible between similar countries. By breaking down the issue into its component parts, the category manager would have been able to distinguish between mirages in some areas and genuine benefits in others.

In similar fashion, one of the interventions made by the group chief executive of the consulting firm also turned out net negative. Determined to get some savings in database costs and unable to win support for a central function, he insisted on a joint project to define state-of-the-art equipment. Led by the group finance director and involving senior managers from each unit, the project team spent many hours agreeing common specifications and evaluating equipment. They even hired a consultant to help. In the final analysis, however, the state-of-the-art equipment offered only marginal improvement to the direct mail efforts.

By devoting more time to disaggregation, the chief executive might have avoided his mistake. By defining the benefits that state-of-the-art equipment could bring, he would have realised that the benefits would be unlikely to pay for the cost of the project team, let alone for new equipment.

While it is not certain that disaggregation would eliminate these examples of net negative interventions, it is clear that disaggregation helps. It helps not only by distinguishing between the different benefits being targeted, each of which might be best addressed by a different intervention, but also by providing the specificity that is needed to resolve conflicts and disagreements.

Framing

Disaggregation helps to provide clarity and focus in benefit definition. But most situations still involve a mix of different benefits. Any attempt to standardise brand positioning will not only achieve this benefit, it will also increase the transfer of know-how. Any attempt to reduce the costs of mailings by centralising database management will also result in some improvement in the sharing of best practice.

In fact, most situations have the potential to deliver multiple benefits. This makes the task of cost/benefit analysis particularly difficult. A com-

plete analysis may involve hard-to-make evaluations of a large number
of different kinds of benefit. Moreover, since different benefits often
require different interventions, there is a danger of trying to develop
interventions aimed at achieving a bundle of different benefits but not
well targeted on any one of them. The chief executive's desire to set up
a central database is a good example of a poorly targeted intervention
bracketing multiple benefits.

But the alternative of designing tailored solutions for each individual
benefit is also awkward. There is a danger of 'analysis paralysis' as disaggregation is taken to a level of detail that cannot be handled. There is
also a danger of cross-effects as an intervention to achieve one benefit
cancels out the effects of a second intervention designed to achieve another. Finally, opportunities to intervene in ways that will achieve a
combination of benefits may be missed.

The solution is what we call 'framing': developing a clarity of purpose
around one or a few related benefits as the primary benefits and relegating the other benefits to secondary status. Often the process of
disaggregation provides alternative ways of framing the issue. Sometimes
additional ways of framing emerge that cut across the original structure of
disaggregation.

The management of international brands could be framed in three
ways that follow the structure of Exhibit 2.1.

1   Making the 'recognisable brand' the primary benefit.
2   Making the 'reduction of duplication and bad practice' the primary
    benefits.
3   Making the 'flow of know-how' the primary benefit.

A fourth way of framing the issue that cuts across the analysis in Exhibit
2.1 is to make cost reduction the primary benefit. In other words: standardise elements of the product and marketing mix not with the aim of
making the brand recognisable but to reduce the costs of ingredients,
packaging, advertising, etc. This option would also involve centralising
some decision-making to reduce the decision burden and the staffing in
the individual countries.

The value of framing the linkage issue around a primary benefit is that it provides focus: focus for thinking about the choice of intervention; focus for estimating the size of the prize; and focus for thinking about why the business units are not already working together to address the opportunity. Framing is a way of pulling the pieces back together around some common theme that will help the decision–maker choose a better intervention.

● The database example ended up becoming a number of different projects each framed around different primary benefits. The first project was a brand-values project that encompassed much more than the mailings. The project involved defining the brand values and ensuring that policies existed not only for mailings, but for many other parts of the business, including consulting reports, recruitment and telephone handling. The second project was a co-ordinated mailing-plan project, designed both to avoid over-mailing some sensitive customers and to reduce costs by combining mailings. The third project was the ill-fated state-of-the-art equipment project, aimed at raising the effectiveness of the direct-mail activities. The fourth project was a cost-reduction exercise, aimed at developing reliable cost data for each business for the purpose of internal benchmarking. The data was then compared to external benchmarks. The surprising conclusion of this analysis was that the smaller businesses were more efficient than the larger business because they did not have a dedicated direct-mail activity (it was carried out by other staff in their spare time). Some changes were therefore made in the management of the larger unit to reduce costs.

Disaggregation and framing are not, however, panaceas. They do not always lead to clear results. In fact, it is possible to remain unclear about the main benefits of a potential linkage even after efforts to disaggregate and frame. The example in the sidebar – 'Building a systems capability' – illustrates this point well. Even after defining the benefits that could be gained from linking an audit business with a strategy-consulting business, managers were still uncertain which were the major benefits or how the linkage issue should be framed. We will say more about uncertainty in Chapter 6, where we deal with exploratory interventions as a way of reducing uncertainty.

Building a systems capability

Corstell Consulting (as we shall call it) is an international auditing and consulting company with sales of more than $300 million. The organisation consists of four different businesses: auditing, including a broad range of accountancy services, technology consulting, strategy consulting, and engineering consultancy.

The issue the firm faced centred on the expansion of the IT-consulting activities of the strategy business. The background is worth describing in some detail. Strategy consulting is a highly attractive business. It involves working on the most pressing top management issues facing companies. Consultants investigate the situation, develop solutions and make recommendations. The business is staffed by the top graduates of the top business schools, who often earn up to 50% more than they would in equivalent industry jobs. Average partner earnings may exceed $1,000,000 a year, and partner-to-staff ratios are less than 1 to 10. The route to partnership is fast and furious. New entrants expect to make partner grade in six years or leave.

In the early 1990s Corstell's strategy-consulting business grew rapidly on the back of two trends – business process re-engineering and strategic systems consulting. As they reviewed their business processes, many companies found they were facing big strategic issues in their information systems. Corstell's strategy business grew fast as the demand for its problem-solving skills and top management perspective increased. Profitability also improved as assignments lengthened, enabling the firm to achieve higher billability. (Billability measures the percentage of time a consultant is billed out to clients versus doing other activities.)

The re-engineering and systems-strategy work drew the strategy business into more and more projects where the client required not only a recommendation but also help in implementing it. In the systems area this meant project-managing new systems and even, on occasions, writing code. The business had begun to recruit different kinds of staff for this work: individuals with technical rather than problem solving skills, and with different career aspirations.

The new systems-implementation work was highly profitable because it involved larger numbers of staff for each partner and higher billability. The strategy business therefore decided to expand its systems department, not only to ensure a fuller client service, but also as a profitable growth opportunity.

The synergy issue concerned the relationship that should exist between the strategy business and the auditing business. The leader of the firm, James Haslet, had been looking for opportunities to create synergy between the two businesses, particularly as the strategy business became more involved in implementation work in areas where the audit business had experience. Haslet wanted to see the audit and strategy businesses work together to develop a systems capability. He argued that the audit business had many technically qualified people who could do systems-implementation work, while the strategy business had client relationships and assignments that would bring in revenues. Because of this belief, he had worked hard to bring the heads of the two businesses together to co-ordinate this opportunity. He had also been instrumental in setting up a joint project team consisting of partners and managers from both businesses to examine the issues.

The project team was making slow progress. Pressure of client assignments and lack of commitment from both sets of partners were to blame. Haslet felt that if he did not make some additional intervention, the opportunity to gain value through co-ordination would slip away.

At first the systems project looked like a very attractive co-ordination opportunity. Both businesses had resources to contribute, and the potential seemed substantial. It had been estimated that billings could be increased by $30 million, just by doing work that was currently being referred to independent systems businesses. However, a different picture emerged as a result of attempts to define the benefits more precisely.

Three alternative framings were discussed.

- Set up a systems business as a joint venture between the two other businesses.
- Set up a systems capability within the audit business to do subcontract work for the strategy business.
- Build a systems capability on to the existing strategy business.

Not surprisingly the two businesses disagreed about the way the issue should be framed. The audit business preferred to see it as an opportunity to develop a systems capability for its own clients which it could then subcontract to the strategy business. The strategy consultants on the other hand viewed the opportunity as a way of expanding their own existing systems capability.

Could the partners resolve the issue by disaggregating and understanding the benefits more clearly? Starting with a common objective they could all agree on – improving firm performance – they defined the main benefit as being to develop a more successful systems capability (Exhibit 2.3). At the same time they noted that there might be some separate benefits from the project to both the audit and strategy businesses, in the form of increased billings or billability.

Exhibit 2.3 Disaggregating the systems capability issue.

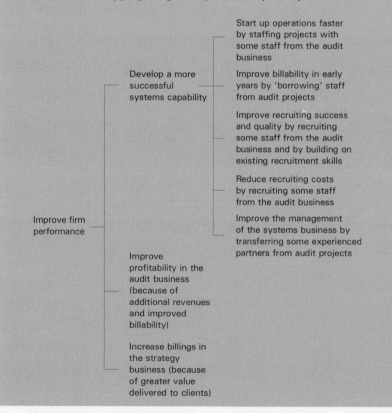

As they examined how co-ordination might help, however, the partners began to realise that there was no obvious big prize. There were a number of small areas of potential benefit with varying degrees of certainty. Most of the benefits would be easier to obtain if the new capability was part of the audit business, but at the possible cost of difficulties between strategy and audit partners. The strategy partners therefore remained unconvinced that the benefits were large enough to justify losing control over their activity.

Haslet was uncertain what to do. He could impose a framing on the problem in the hope that this would un-jam the discussions; he could get closely involved himself to try and resolve the differences; or he could conclude it was an issue that the businesses had to resolve between themselves. In the end he chose the latter course because he could not identify a prize big enough to warrant any major interference.

The advice we give in this section may seem rather straightforward to many readers. Yet we have observed that it is difficult to do well. Linkage issues are frequently inadequately framed, causing confusion not only in the minds of business-level managers but also in the minds of parent managers. Given the pervasive influence of the synergy bias, managers who think carefully about framing the issues and looking for targeted interventions almost invariably make better decisions than those who do not. Managers who deal in broad aggregates and vague definitions find it much harder to combat the synergy bias.

Sizing the prize

The third practical technique is estimating the size of the benefit. Without some sense of the size or importance of the likely benefits, the decision maker is uncertain how much effort to put into the intervention. Moreover, given the concerns raised in Chapter 1, parent managers would be wise to avoid initiatives that yield small benefits (except under particular conditions – see Chapter 6).

In principle, estimating the size of the benefit is a matter of cost-benefit analysis. However, accurate cost-benefit analysis is difficult to do. As a result, it is often overlooked entirely – with the consequence that many anticipated benefits turn out to be mirages. Our advice is to accept that accurate cost-benefit analysis is not achievable. Instead, we suggest an order-of-magnitude judgement and a strategic assessment. But first we will summarise why precise cost-benefit analysis for synergy interventions is so hard to carry out.

Cost-benefit analysis involves assessing primary benefits, secondary benefits, direct costs and indirect costs (Exhibit 2.4). Each element, with the possible exception of direct costs, is hard to estimate.

Exhibit 2.4   Cost/benefit analysis.

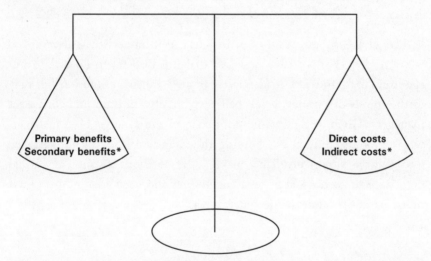

*There is an overlap in our language between the term *knock-on effects* and the terms *secondary benefits* and *indirect costs*. The value of the additional concept of knock-on effects (Chapter 5) is that it brings special attention to four kinds of effect that are often overlooked.

Primary benefits are frequently uncertain. How many additional sales will accrue from standardising the presentation of a brand across different countries? What costs will be eliminated through efforts to reduce duplication? What bottom-line benefits will result from transferring best practice? Sometimes managers can answer these questions from experience, but often they cannot: market response to a standardised brand is hard to forecast; the cost impact of reduced duplication may depend on unpredictable local management decisions; the applicability of best practice from one unit to another can be contentious. Whatever the reason, it is comparatively rare for managers to be able to place firm numbers on a benefit, and it is not uncommon for them to debate whether a benefit exists at all. The same is true for secondary benefits. Secondary benefits are no different in nature from primary benefits and suffer from the same estimation uncertainties.

Direct costs include out-of-pocket expenses and management time that will be devoted to the initiative. Of all the items in a cost-benefit analysis, these are usually the easiest to judge. Estimates can be made of expenses and management time with some expectation of accuracy. Indirect costs, however, are much more difficult to judge.

Indirect costs consist of opportunity costs (the value that is lost from not doing something else with the management time) and compromise costs (the value that is lost from having to make decisions that are not the optimum for some businesses). Both are factors present in most synergy interventions, often underrated ones. We will therefore devote some space to explaining what we mean.

Opportunity costs

Opportunity costs exist where scarce resources are involved. Management time, particularly that of senior line managers, is normally one of an organisation's scarcest resources. In our experience, the single biggest cause of hostility towards linkage initiatives is the perceived opportunity cost. The business managers simply believe they have better things to do with their time.

Too often we meet parent managers who do not give enough consideration to opportunity costs. They pile one corporate initiative on top of another, without recognising that the business managers are not only sinking under the burden of extra tasks – they are beginning to devote too little time to their customers, products or organisational processes. Opportunity costs are ever present and often large.

● The project team assembled to choose state-of-the-art database equipment encountered a classic opportunity-cost problem. Since the team was led by the finance director and comprised exclusively of senior people from each of the businesses, the opportunity costs – the value these managers could have been creating if they had done something else with their time – was large. Even if they had been able to find equipment that created a big improvement in mailing effectiveness, it might still not have been worth the opportunity cost.

● In the international brand example, the opportunity cost of the squabbles between Germany, France and the UK about the standards for the noodle product far outweighed the benefits of standardisation. This would have been the case, even if the markets had been more similar. One of the problems with opportunity costs is that they are harder to recognise from the perspective of the parent manager than the business manager who is in the thick of them. Frequently, foot-dragging by the business manager, interpreted as NIH by the impatient parent manager, is in reality a genuine clash of priorities.

● In another example, the head of an industrial-paints division was having problems persuading his French business to accept a new technology that had been commercialised in the company's home country, Germany. The division head was beginning to lose patience with what he felt was the 'not-invented-here' attitudes of the French managers.

   From the French perspective, the issue looked different. 'We recognise that this is currently a better technology, and we will probably need to change', explained the French business head. 'But we are currently making other changes in our organisation and I don't want to confuse the initiatives. Moreover, my research people sincerely believe their technology will prove to be superior, and I feel I must give them another year to prove or disprove their case.'

The French manager could see two major opportunity costs. First, senior management time devoted to switching technology would detract from the time needed to make 'other changes in the organisation'. Second, changing the technology would prevent the research staff from testing the alternative technology, and the French manager judged that this would be more valuable than a year's delay.

Eventually, frustrated by what he saw as French bloody-mindedness, the division head insisted that the French manager change technology. By this time, the French company had completed the other changes. It had also discovered that the alternative technology was not in fact superior. The French manager was therefore ready to comply with his boss's instruction. The overall result was satisfactory. But because the division manager had misunderstood the nature of the opportunity costs involved, he drew the wrong lesson from the experience. In future, he was determined to be more forceful when faced with resistance. The lesson he should have learnt was to be more patient if the cause of resistance is opportunity costs.

One of the most important calls for parent managers to make in deciding to intervene is the size of the opportunity costs. Interventions change the priorities on the 'to-do' list of the business managers involved. Pushing a linkage initiative higher up the to-do list inevitably pushes other items further down. Unless the intervening manager understand this, there is a danger opportunity costs will exceed the net benefits of the linkage: the value lost by relegating some items in the priority list will outweigh the value created by promoting the synergy initiative to the top.

Yet opportunity costs are hard to estimate. The opportunity cost is the loss of net benefits from other initiatives. Not only is it difficult to know exactly which initiatives will now get less attention, it is also hard to know how the reduction in attention will translate into a reduction in benefit. The net benefits of these other initiatives are as hard to calculate as the net benefits of the linkage being promoted. In other words, opportunity costs are even harder to assess than benefits.

Opportunity costs exist not only for business–unit managers but also for parent managers too. Any intervention that requires the time of parent managers, particularly that of the CEO, has high opportunity costs. Every treatise on the subject of change management explains that change initiatives are more successful the more they are supported by the CEO. As a result, the CEO's 'active support' is one of the scarcest resources a corporation has. The opportunity cost of the time spent by corporate centre managers needs to be included. What other initiatives would the corporate centre managers be pursuing? What value will be lost if these initiatives are given lower priority?

In describing opportunity costs, we have focused on the scarce time and attention of managers and the degree to which this is diverted from other priorities. We should also recognise that there may be other scarce resources. For example, the number of new products that can be launched in any period, the number of visits a customer will agree to in any period, and the capacity of scarce machinery are all scarce resources that have high opportunity costs.

Compromise costs

Compromise costs are associated with choosing between two incompatible outcomes. For example, choosing to use an international rather than an established local brand will advance the development of the international brand, but at the cost of lower sales of some products in some locations. Choosing to rationalise production from three plants to one will have benefits in the form of increased margins, but may also create compromise costs reducing service levels for one or more of the units. It will certainly result in some loss of flexibility and increase in distance between marketing and manufacturing in some units.

In our experience, compromise costs are less frequently overlooked by parent managers than opportunity costs. In the international-brand example, the category managers were fully aware of the potential compromise costs of imposing international standards on local product launches. Most of the category managers had experienced the problems that arise when one marketing campaign is developed for two or more different market segments, or when one sales force is asked to sell different kinds of products: the marketing campaign or sales efforts inevitably suit one market or one product better than others. These represent compromise costs that must be offset against the savings.

The database co-ordination example earlier in this chapter also involved compromise costs. If two mailings go out in one envelope the slight loss of impact for each must be offset against the potential savings. If one central team manages the direct-mail activities, clashes of priority will occur. Two businesses will want the department's urgent attention at the same time, and one or other will suffer a compromise cost.

The problem with compromise costs is not lack of recognition but the difficulty of estimating their impact. What is the loss of impact from the joint mailing? How much is too much? What is the disadvantage of having one marketing campaign? What is the consequence of a delay while another business unit gets priority? Many of these questions can be answered with enough data and experimentation. But the information is rarely available at the time when a decision needs to be made.

Order-of-magnitude estimates

We have taken a number of pages to explain that sizing the prize is not easy. Benefits are hard to pin down and so are costs, particularly opportunity and compromise costs. Accurate cost/benefit analysis is not a realistic proposition.

The only solution is order-of-magnitude estimates. Are the potential benefits £1 million, £10 million or £100 million? Are the costs likely to be significant in relation to the benefits? This is not science. This is back-of-the-envelope stuff. What, to the nearest zero, are the benefits likely to be? What percentage of this figure should be taken off to allow for costs? What, to the nearest zero, is left?

Order-of-magnitude estimates are most useful when measured in terms of overall impact on the businesses involved. Profit (e.g. 1% increase, 10% increase, or 100% increase) or return on sales (e.g improve ROS by 0.1%, 1% or 5%) are useful measures of overall impact. Another useful order-of-magnitude measure is shareholder value. What will be the impact on shareholder value of this collaboration: £1 million, £10 million or £100 million?

● The category manager for cookies in the international food company wanted to kick-start the process of creating some international cookie brands. Initially he encouraged the marketing managers to visit each other and identify products that could be transferred from one country to another. Some products were transferred, particularly from the USA to Europe, but the brand names and brand positionings were changed. After some years of frustration, the category manager decided to make an intervention. He persuaded the US business (with a good deal of pressure) to launch one of the more successful European products, using the European brand name and positioning.

When we did an order of magnitude estimate of the size of the prize, we got a shock: the net benefit, we discovered, was probably negative (Exhibit 2.5). Managers expected the new product to be successful, although they recognised that it would not be a major force in the market. We estimated that it might perform as well as the US company's average product launch; in other words create about $5 million in shareholder value. In addition there would be some secondary benefits: managers would learn more about the US market, and, if the product was successful, it would tend to improve relationships between European and US companies.

Since the direct costs of the product marketing and related expenses had been deducted in arriving at the $5 million figure, we only had to estimate the indirect opportunity and compromise costs. There were clearly opportunity costs: retailers would only accept a few new products, and the company had traditionally limited itself to five product launches a year. By choosing to launch the European cookie, the company was choosing not to launch an alternative. We were tempted therefore to estimate the opportunity cost as the loss in value from not launching the typical worst performing new product. The worst performer was usually a net value destroyer, producing around $2 million of negative shareholder value. Adding back that figure to the positive European contribution (because it would have been saved) would have given a revised estimate for the size of the prize as $7 million.

However, when we asked the US marketing managers whether they could confidently predict in advance which would be the worst performer among their product launches, the answer was no. We therefore had to estimate the opportunity cost as being the value of the average product launch (i.e. plus $5 million). We also recorded a further opportunity cost; the learning and market knowledge that would have been gained from launching some other product.

In addition, we had to reckon on some compromise costs. The requirement that the new product be launched with the same brand and positioning as in Europe meant that it would be somewhat less successful than if it had been positioned especially for the US market. We judged that the compromise cost might reduce the value created by 20%, or $1 million in shareholder value.

We therefore ended up with an estimate of the size of the prize as follows: destruction of about $1 million in shareholder value in return for the benefits that relationships might improve between the US and European marketing teams, and of being able to point to at least one international cookie brand. When presented like this the 'synergy' initiative looked pretty unattractive.

Exhibit 2.5   Estimating the size of the prize for launch of European product. (Numbers and text in brackets implies a negative.)

Costs and benefits	Impact
Primary benefits less direct costs	$5 million
Indirect benefits	Information about the market Improve US/Europe relations
Opportunity costs	($5 million) (Information about the market for a different product)
Compromise costs	($1 million)
Net Impact	($1 million) Improved US/Europe relations

Order of magnitude quantification is, in our view, an essential step in making good synergy decisions. As the example demonstrates, it is easy to assume that the benefits are greater than the costs. Quantification is needed to confirm the cost-benefit intuition. Quantification is also necessary to allay the concerns of managers who are reluctant to pursue the opportunity or who are focused on other priorities. Without a comprehensive reckoning of the costs and benefits, the initiative ends up being sold to the organisation as a matter of principle or as a strategic necessity: much better to sell it as a sound commercial decision that will bring substantially more benefit than costs.

Strategic assessment

Alongside the order-of-magnitude financial judgement, it is also useful to make a broad strategic assessment. What is the strategic importance of this initiative? Where does it rank on a list of strategic priorities?

The value of the strategic assessment is two-fold. First, it provides a useful check on the financial assessment. An initiative that has a big financial impact ought to have high strategic importance and vice versa. The order-of-magnitude financial estimate and the strategic assessment ought to come to the same answer. Second, the strategic assessment provides a useful indication of the opportunity costs. An initiative that has low strategic importance is likely to have relatively high opportunity costs compared with the benefits: the loss of value from pushing a low-priority item up the 'to-do' list is normally greater than the gain.

In some circumstances, an initiative with low strategic importance has low opportunity costs too. This occurs when the initiative does not consume any scarce resources. If the initiative does not require the attention of senior managers in the parent organisation or the businesses, opportunity costs will be small even if the strategic importance is low. We will say more about small benefit synergies in Chapter 6.

A strategic assessment should take into account not just the position of the company as a whole, but that of each of the participant units. What is the strategic importance of the initiative for each of the business units, and what for the corporate parent? The decision maker needs to understand the opportunity costs that each participant is facing to be able to identify the most suitable intervention.

● In the cookie example, the creation of an international cookie brand was clearly not a strategic priority for either of the businesses involved. Both took part in the new product launch because the category manager believed it was important. The category manager, on the other hand, clearly felt that the creation of an international cookie brand was an important corporate priority. It wasn't until he was faced with the financial analysis that he began to question his corporate-level strategic assessment. Because the two assessments arrived at different answers, he was obliged to challenge his strategic judgement. He ultimately abandoned the attempt to create international cookie brands.

Just posing the question about strategic importance can be enough to identify a mirage or pinpoint weak logic. If the chief executive in the database case had stopped to ask himself how strategically important it was to upgrade his hardware, he would have come up with a low score: incremental improvement in the management of mailings was not an important issue for any of his three businesses. It was only important to the chief executive because he was actively looking for synergy opportunities. A strategic assessment is another way of helping to spot mirages such as these.

In summary, we have two pieces of advice concerning strategic assessments. First, beware of situations where one or more of the businesses involved in the initiative rates it low on strategic importance. Not only does this mean that managers will starve it of attention, it also means that the parent manager may be looking at a mirage. Second, compare the strategic assessment with the order–of–magnitude financial estimate. If the two don't match, revisit both analyses. By using both methods of sizing the prize, parent managers can be more confident of their judgements.

Summary

Synergy initiatives are frequently dogged by uncertainty about costs and benefits. This is often offered as an excuse for inadequate thought and analysis. We suggest that sizing the prize is essential, even if only in order-of-magnitude terms.

Sizing the prize is important because of the correction it brings to mental biases. The synergy bias causes parent managers to assume that there are net benefits when, as in the cookie case, some quite simple analysis demonstrates the reverse. The parenting presumption causes parent managers to assume that resistance from business managers is motivated more by NIH than by evaluation of costs and benefits. Careful consideration of opportunity and compromise costs, complemented by an assessment of the strategic importance of the initiative to the businesses, can help parent managers distinguish between justified and unjustified resistance. In other words, effort devoted to clarifying the primary benefit, disaggregating to a lower level of detail if necessary, and estimating the net financial and strategic impact is a necessary discipline to help offset the mental biases.

● One manager proposed setting up a central unit to help manage his company's efforts to develop electronic media products. The group consisted of a number of magazine, newspaper and exhibition businesses, each of which had opportunities to create products or services from the new CD-ROM, on-line, internet and IT based media. Since the manager was asking for an annual investment of more than £200,000 in the unit, we asked him why he was not presenting a cost/benefit analysis.

'If I treated this as a business proposal and went in with estimates of revenues and what not, I would get torn to shreds. They would get stuck into the detail of the numbers and I would be laughed out of the room. I have to sell this as an issue of commitment. Are we committed to these new media opportunities or not? If we are, £200,000 is a small price to pay for giving our efforts a leg up.'

This kind of decision-making process contains all the features that lead to poorly thought-out interventions and energetic pursuit of mirages.

- What precisely is the benefit of creating a central unit: devoting more management time to important issues; improving the technical skills of managers; the ability to co-ordinate learning and experience; or what?
- What can the centre contribute that would not happen if the businesses are left to their own devices, and what financial benefits might this bring? Is this a mirage?
- Which of these technologies has most potential? Why is a central unit the best way to support development for all of them? Why don't we have a different, tailored solution for each technology?
- What costs, beyond direct expenses, will this unit impose on the organisation in terms of additional points of contact, meetings, information gathering, disagreements, etc.?

These are all areas of uncertainty. But it is folly to use uncertainty as a reason for ignoring the questions. The mental discipline of defining the benefit is designed to avoid this folly. The habits of disaggregating, framing and sizing the prize ensure that the parent manager does not need to make decisions on generalisations such as 'commitment to electronic media'. Instead, decisions can be made on clearer definitions of the benefits, such as 'increase the number of new CD-ROMs issued by 50% and double the success rate'.

Gaining clarity does not necessarily eliminate uncertainty. We may know that the primary potential benefit is increased success with CD-ROMs, but we may still be highly uncertain about whether that success can be achieved. In this chapter, we duck the uncertainty problem in order to sell the mental discipline of 'sizing the prize'. In chapter 6, we address the issue head on. Our recommendation is to choose 'exploratory' rather than 'implementation' interventions. Parent managers faced with high levels of uncertainty should, we argue, choose interventions whose primary objective is to deliver information and learning rather than final results; and we suggest that this requires a mental approach that is different from a normal implementation approach.

3

Pinpoint the Parenting Opportunity

There is no reason for managers in the parent company to intervene unless something is stopping business unit managers from doing the commercially sensible thing. Parenting opportunities occur because business managers

- have not perceived the benefits
- have mis-evaluated the size of the benefits
- are not motivated to help create the benefits
- do not have the capabilities or mechanisms to create the benefits.

In each of these four areas of parenting opportunity there are different 'causes' of the opportunity and different 'roles' for parent managers to play. By pinpointing the opportunity, parent managers can clarify the role they need to play and identify possible interventions that would be beneficial.

In this chapter, we want to explain more fully what we mean by 'pinpointing the parenting opportunity' and to show why this mental discipline is vital in our approach to the management of synergies. We begin with a fundamental question: why and when should the corporate parent take a hand in managing links between its businesses at all? We then discuss different sorts of opportunities to intervene – 'parenting opportunities', in our terminology. By helping managers to understand the reasons why they might need to intervene, we hope also to make clear the implications for their own role. We conclude the chapter with some advice on how to use this mental discipline to shape the interventions that the parent makes.

The parenting opportunity concept

In deciding what the parent should do to promote synergy in its portfolio, what assumptions should we make about the intentions and capabilities of the management teams of the business units involved? Should we assume that business managers are generally blind to good opportunities, uninterested in improving their performance, incapable of reaching win-win agreements with other units, and mired in fundamentally unco-operative, not-invented-here (NIH) attitudes? Or should we assume that the businesses are run by managers who are anxious to find and pursue any opportunities that will help them to achieve their performance targets, and are able and willing to co-operate with other units, either within or outside the company?

These extremes may provide an unrealistically black or white choice, and most business managers probably fall somewhere in the middle of the spectrum. Nevertheless, we believe that although the first set of assumptions ('blind, incapable, NIH') is usually wrong, it underlies most corporate efforts to get businesses to work together. This explains the 'parenting presumption' – the belief that intervention is the natural job of parent managers. We believe that the second set of assumptions ('enthusiastic, able, willing') is a safer starting point, and provides a much firmer basis for deciding whether, when and how the parent should get involved.

If we assume business units are able and willing, we can expect them to exploit most of the synergy opportunities on offer. Only if they cannot see a potential benefit, or are not motivated or able to capitalise on the opportunity, will their spontaneous decisions not be enough. In consequence, instead of intervening as a matter of course, corporate parents should only take a hand if they believe that the businesses' own decisions are not yielding all the benefits available, and if they can identify actions on their own part that will release benefits that the businesses cannot achieve on their own.

A parenting opportunity exists therefore when, and only when:

• there are linkage benefits that will not be realised by the businesses collaborating in a natural self-interested way;
• there is a role for the parent in helping to obtain the benefits.

The parent's role may involve removing blockages that are preventing the businesses from seeing or acting on opportunities to work together, or may call for interventions that increase the benefits or reduce the costs of collaboration (see Exhibit 3.1).

Exhibit 3.1   Parenting roles.

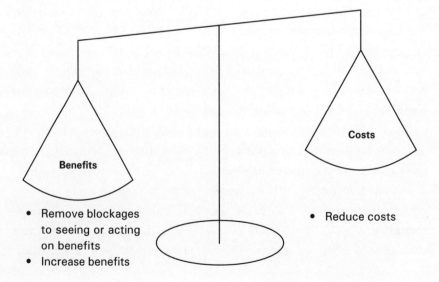

• Remove blockages to seeing or acting on benefits
• Increase benefits

• Reduce costs

The implication of this view of parenting opportunities should be spelled out. Unless the parent has a clear idea of the parenting opportunity it is targeting, it should not intervene. For example, two businesses with common customers may not be collaborating in serving them. But that doesn't necessarily mean that the parent should take action. It should only do so if it can see obstacles that are getting in the way of the businesses working together or actions it could take to improve the cost-benefit trade-off from doing so. To intervene without understanding the parenting opportunity can only succeed by accident. More likely, it will waste time and energy – destroying value rather than creating it.

Practically, an emphasis on parenting opportunities can steer parent managers away from the sort of hopeful but non-specific interventions that cause so much frustration to business units. On the positive side, it can also give a much clearer focus for selecting promising interventions.

At the same time, the parenting opportunity logic provides a fundamental intellectual rationale for the centre's role in the management of synergies. By accepting that the centre normally has no call to take action, it builds the justification for intervention around exceptions – specific situations in which, for a variety of reasons, spontaneous co-operation between the business units may be weak or non-existent. It is in these circumstances that parent managers can intervene with the confidence that they are addressing real synergy opportunities and not mirages.

Types of parenting opportunity

In our research, we have encountered many different parenting opportunities, each with its own implications for the role to be played by the parent. To provide structure and guidance on where to search for parenting opportunities, we divide them into four categories, each requiring a different type of parental role: perception opportunities, evaluation opportunities, motivation opportunities, and implementation opportunities (see Exhibit 3.2).

The four categories correspond to different steps in bringing linkages to fruition.

Exhibit 3.2 Four types of parenting opportunities.

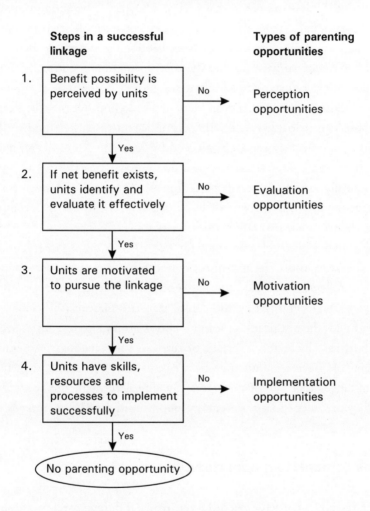

- First, the units must perceive a potentially rewarding opportunity. If they are overlooking potential benefits, there may be a role for the parent in helping them to see the possibilities.
- Second, the units must evaluate the opportunity correctly – if they don't, they will not be able to identify the net benefit. If there are biases or errors in their evaluations, there may be a role for the parent in removing them.

- Third, the units involved must all be motivated to pursue the opportunity. If one or more units are reluctant, the parent may have a role in adjusting incentives and/or outcomes to align motivations with the group interests.
- Lastly, the units must have the skills, processes and management resources in place to allow them to exploit the opportunity successfully. If they lack these means, there may be a role for the parent to help with implementation in some way.

Thus, there can be different sorts of parenting opportunities for each step in realising a synergy benefit. If, on the other hand, the units are able to complete all the steps satisfactorily on their own, parental involvement is unnecessary. There is no parenting opportunity and no need for the parent to take action.

In the next four sections of the chapter, we discuss each of the four types of parenting opportunity in more detail.

Perception opportunities

The first requirement for achieving synergies is that the units involved should perceive the possibility of benefits. Units should be constantly scanning for possible benefits and focusing in on areas which may have potential.

Our baseline assumption is that competent managers will be devoting what they believe is an appropriate level of effort to this scanning task. They will balance the likelihood of unearthing possible benefits against the costs of digging for them. For example, a product-group head in one country may decide to spend more time finding out what is going on in his product group in other countries than on briefing himself about other product groups. This judgement would reflect a belief that sharing opportunities across countries within the product group are likely to be much more fruitful than with other product groups. Weighing up uncertain benefits against hard-to-quantify opportunity costs and other scanning costs is not easy, but business managers, daily engaged with the details of their businesses, should normally be better placed to make the trade-offs than parent managers.

There are, however, circumstances in which business managers may fail to scan for opportunities in the most productive way. If we can identify what causes a business manager to overlook potential benefits, we are well on the way to finding corresponding roles for the parent. The nature of perception opportunities, and the implied roles for the parent, are summarised in Exhibit 3.3.

Exhibit 3.3 Perception parenting opportunities.

Causes	Roles for parent
Lack of interest	Reduce inertia, parochialism, bias
Lack of information	Improve accessibility, relevance, comparability of information
Lack of personal contacts	Facilitate network building
Costs of scanning	Reduce scanning costs
Hard-to-perceive opportunities	Help to identify
• collective benefits	• group perspective
• special scanning skills needed	• scanning specialists
• require radical new initiatives	• champion the initiative

Lack of interest

Despite our baseline assumption, not all business managers are genuinely interested in seeking out synergies. The desire for an easy life, lack of ambition, or simply inertia make some managers unwilling to look beyond the boundaries of their own businesses. Some managers are so parochial or blinkered that they either fail to scan at all or self-servingly misinterpret the results. These distortions may apply to co-ordination in general, or may be focused on specific topics. For example, a previous bad experience with sharing a sales force may make a manager totally unwilling to contemplate any similar initiative, whatever its merits.

Where managers seem uninterested in looking for opportunities to work together, the parent can play a useful role in reducing inertia, parochialism or bias. In Rentokil, for example, branch managers are under considerable pressure to seek out best practice from elsewhere in the company. Their performance reviews expose any areas of the business in which performance is below that of sister units, and branch managers who do not pick up good ideas from elsewhere are exposed. Because branch managers are only too aware of the pressure to find new ways of improving their businesses, few of them lack interest in learning or looking for other linkage benefits from their colleagues in other branches.

If parent managers believe that business managers are uninterested in finding synergies, they need to understand why. Then they can design an intervention that attacks the cause. If the problem is inertia, the answer may be tougher targets and sharper incentives. If it is a matter of overconfidence and unjustified self-belief, marshalling evidence to the contrary may be the right response – although eventually it may need a change in management. If the root cause is a fundamental belief that the businesses have little to share and that searching for synergies is a waste of time, the parent may need to do more of the scanning itself (always assuming that the business managers are wrong). There are many possible reasons for lack of interest and an even larger number of ways to address them. But the starting point in designing an intervention must be a close understanding of the cause of the problem.

Lack of information

In large multi-business companies, with many different units, often geographically spread around the world, it is impossible for business managers to know everything that is going on in other units. This basic problem – too much information for people to take in – is greatly compounded if the units put together information in indigestible forms, if reporting systems use information that is not readily comparable across units, and if a culture of secrecy discourages managers from obtaining information on sister units. Lack of a free flow of relevant, comparable, user-friendly information often prevents otherwise co-operative management teams from linking up.

Parents have many options for improving information flow. Most basically, they can insist on common definitions of terms and reporting criteria for all units. This is no trivial task: multi-business companies such as ABB, which has 5000 separate profit centres, have invested hundreds of millions of dollars to develop common information systems. Alternatively, the parent can promote benchmarking exercises, forums for information exchange, manuals that document key practices and processes, and groupware, such as Lotus Notes, that encourage the sharing of information. As with 'lack of interest', the interventions chosen to address 'lack of information' must take account of the specific blockages or inhibitions that need to be overcome.

Lack of personal contacts

Given the difficulty of cutting through all the available information, direct discussion with a trusted colleague in a sister unit is often an excellent short cut. Such a contact can help to pick out opportunities for linkage and to zero in on the information needed to check them out. But this route is only open to managers who have a personal network of contacts across company boundaries. In multinational companies, where unit managers are located in different countries, operate in different cultures, and speak different languages, personal networks are difficult to establish.

It is for this reason that companies such as Mars and Unilever devote an otherwise surprising amount of corporate energy to the fostering of personal networks. They plan career moves to expose managers to colleagues in a range of businesses, they support visits, meetings and cross-company task force activities, and they strongly encourage managers to develop personal contact with colleagues elsewhere. In Mars, for example, it is part of every manufacturing manager's MBO targets to visit a number of other Mars units every year to identify better practices and build personal networks.

On specific issues, such as how best to approach a shared customer, the parent can often usefully intervene by the simple means of bringing people together and making introductions. In one defence company, we were told how reluctant the different businesses had been to share their customer contacts in developing countries. The businesses had been unwilling to put names into a common corporate database, since they were unsure how their colleagues would use these contacts. Only after the corporate parent arranged a series of social functions to allow people to get to know each other better did managers of the different businesses become confident enough to divulge information on their key contacts. While the parent's intervention may sometimes be targeted on general network building, it can also be prompted by a particular benefit that is being overlooked.

Costs of scanning

Scanning for synergy opportunities is not a costless activity. The direct costs and, even more, the opportunity costs of extensive scanning dictate selectivity. For a marketing manager in a small country such as Belgium, Venezuela or Thailand, the costs of finding out about new product launches, advertising campaigns, or channel tactics in all the other territories of the world may be prohibitive. Even if managers are interested and plugged in, and information is available, the high costs of scanning may prevent them from perceiving linkage opportunities.

The parenting opportunity in these situations is to find ways of reducing the costs of scanning. This may be through making information on other units easier and cheaper to obtain. It therefore overlaps with the roles associated with lack of information, but with the emphasis on making it quicker and less costly for the units to discover what they need to know about each other.

An alternative, and stronger, intervention is for the parent to allocate some scanning responsibilities to a central staff group. The use of a central resource to search for and pass on worthwhile ideas eliminates duplication and takes advantage of economies of scale – allowing, for example, the recruitment of specialists in particular fields. By these means, the parent can reduce scanning costs.

For example the central technology function at 3M has set up a central database listing all of 3M's technology projects. This database, consisting of hundreds of projects, gets updated as projects pass certain milestones – the project launch, the development phase, product launch, etc. It is a low cost way for technical directors to access the breadth of 3M's technology. The cost, for each technical director, to keep tabs on all projects he or she is interested in is an order of magnitude less than it could be if the database did not exist.

Setting up a corporate scanning group makes particular sense for companies with a large number of small units. This is often true in multinationals that operate in many different countries. In these circumstances, the cost of comprehensive scanning for each individual unit may seem prohibitively high compared with the expected benefits. But a corporate expert, working on behalf of all the units, may be able to identify potential benefits much more cost effectively.

Hard-to-perceive opportunities

Some synergy benefits, although worthwhile, are intrinsically hard for the units to perceive. For example, if all units standardise on a particular component and/or supplier, it may be possible to negotiate an attractive group discount. But the size of the discount to any individual unit may not be large enough to persuade it to take the lead in pushing for standardisation, especially given that some units may well resist the move, preferring to choose their own components and suppliers. Even though there may be a substantial collective benefit, it will be difficult for the individual units to see it.

Other situations call for special scanning skills that the units are unlikely to possess. Opportunities to share technical know-how or resources may exist, but will only be apparent to highly qualified engineers of a calibre that few, if any, units possess. Cooper Industries, for example, uses the specialist expertise of its manufacturing services staff to identify process improvements that could be applicable elsewhere in the company.

In some cases, the opportunity may require a radical new initiative that no individual unit would be likely to contemplate. At Pearson, the media and publishing company, the back office operations of nearly all the UK subsidiaries, such as Longman, Addison Wesley, Penguin, Pearson Professional and the Financial Times, are being combined into a single shared operation. This will yield savings of more than £10 million a year, with no reduction in customer service. But it will involve a complete change in the value chains of the businesses, a reduction in the scope of operations under the direct control of each business, and large-scale redundancies. For obvious reasons, it is highly unlikely that the units themselves would have embarked on this initiative without a strong push from the centre. It would have required too much knowledge about other units' operations, and it would have been too radical a departure, too far beyond the *status quo*, to get onto the agenda of individual units, even if they were searching assiduously for linkage opportunities.

Since enlightened self-interest will not bring such hard-to-perceive opportunities to the surface, the parent's role in these cases must be to take the initiative. This may involve senior line executives or central experts, who can bring a group perspective to the identification of collective benefits or generate new insights about where benefits could exist. Or it may call for setting up a task force to look into some radical new initiative. At Pearson, the back office reorganisation was an idea that stemmed from the corporate head office. It was followed up by a task force, led by a senior corporate line manager, but involving representatives from all the businesses, along with external consultants, to help put flesh on the bones of the idea. With hard-to-perceive opportunities, the parent needs to go beyond facilitating contacts between the businesses and must take more proactive steps.

Evaluation opportunities

Once managers have spotted a linkage opportunity, the second step in exploiting it is for the units to evaluate it correctly. Will the joint action actually yield significant net value? After taking account of all the direct and indirect costs, will the group gain or lose from following through the idea? In practice, the perception phase is not clearly separate from the evaluation phase, since the initial trawl for opportunities will involve some screening for expected costs and benefits. But we are focusing now on the considered evaluation of opportunities that have made it through the first perception screen.

Again, we reiterate our belief that competent unit managers will, generally, be better placed to evaluate cost benefit trade-offs than parent managers. Not only are the latter more remote from the day-to-day reality of the situation, they often introduce their own biases into evaluations. Normally, we should rely on the judgement of business managers in evaluating whether a proposed linkup is worth doing or not.

Nevertheless, parenting opportunities can arise in the evaluation process. Why and how are shown in Exhibit 3.4.

Exhibit 3.4 Evaluation parenting opportunities.

Causes	Roles for parent
Biases arising from	Rectify bias
• business's experience	• counterbalance to business's experience
• systematic errors	
• business or corporate strategies	• evaluation methods and processes
	• clarify corporate strategy/ philosophy
Costs of evaluation	Reduce evaluation costs
Hard-to-evaluate opportunities	Help to evaluate
• collective benefits	• group perspective
• benefits that depend on initiatives by the parent	• assessment by the parent
• uncertain benefits and costs	• weighing uncertainty, risk and reward

Bias

Corporate parents intent on pushing through synergy initiatives frequently complain that their business units are biased. NIH, bloody-mindedness, or undue protectiveness, they complain, are the reasons why business units fail to assess the benefits correctly. Our contention, on the other hand, is that these criticisms are frequently unjustified, having more to do with a corporate bias in favour of pursuing mirages than with a business unit bias against synergies. But we do accept that there are circumstances in which the businesses may discount the possible rewards of synergy.

Bias against synergy can result from the business's previous experiences. Under pressure from the corporate chief executive, the business units in one professional-service firm had searched repeatedly for 'synergies' from joint product or client development activities. But the differences between the services meant that almost all these initiatives failed. New proposals for collaborative activities tended therefore to be viewed with extreme scepticism, whatever their merits. Managers who have had repeated bad experiences with previous synergy initiatives may become biased against all future proposals.

Bias can also result from the approach used to evaluate proposals. A failure to size potential benefits, or to take account of indirect benefits or costs, for example, may lead to the wrong conclusions. In a retail group, the value of shared purchasing was only accepted after the corporate centre had insisted that the businesses stop debating the principles of collaboration and quantify the discounts available. Working together on the assessment not only showed how much money was at stake, but also yielded spin-off benefits in the shape of better shared understanding, resulting in closer co-ordination of the businesses' strategies. The original approach to evaluation was neither quantitative enough to show up the direct benefits nor broad enough to recognise the indirect benefits that would flow from closer contact between the businesses. If there are systematic errors in the way businesses evaluate synergy opportunities, a bias – whether for or against collaboration – will be the result.

A further important source of bias stems from the strategies of the businesses. Part of the purpose of defining a strategy is establishing priorities. Each business's strategy will necessarily emphasise some issues and de-emphasise others. If managers see that the proposed action contributes to the priority tasks and targets, they will naturally view it favourably. If not, they will give more weight to the opportunity costs.

Where the businesses' evaluations of synergy opportunities are biased, the role for the parent is to correct the distortion. This may require a sustained campaign to overcome hostility arising from previous failures; or it may require managers to develop new evaluation methods. It may even call for a reassessment of business strategies. In a publishing company, the corporate centre was concerned that the different businesses were giving too little attention to opportunities for collaboration in the use of new media, mainly because the businesses' strategies were not particularly focused on new media developments. Rather than zeroing in directly on the new media issue, however, the parent called for a basic reappraisal of strategies by the businesses, in the expectation that this would lead to new priorities that would unleash fresh enthusiasm for new media collaborations. This apparently indirect approach recognised the importance of the businesses' underlying strategies in conditioning the evaluation of opportunities.

Costs of evaluation

As with scanning, the evaluation of opportunities is not a costless process. Implicitly or explicitly, these costs need to be factored into the overall assessment of whether a given collaboration effort is worthwhile. While unlikely to tip the balance, evaluation costs can often reduce the attractiveness of proceeding.

Where evaluation calls for time consuming data gathering and analysis in the businesses, there may be a case for the parent stepping in to take advantage of economies of scale or specialisation. Supply chain rationalisation across many separate national units has yielded large benefits for many companies in recent years. However, analysis and evaluation of possible options is a major task which is liable to distract unit managers from other priorities. Corporate staff or external consultants can relieve the burden.

Hard-to-evaluate opportunities

Some opportunities are intrinsically hard for business managers to evaluate. Where, for example, standardisation of procedures or products will lead to collective benefits, individual units are poorly placed to evaluate their size. A group view is needed. Equally, where the benefits are contingent on some initiative that the parent will take, the parent rather than the individual units will be better able to judge the likely net results. (These sorts of situation also give rise to 'perception opportunities', as discussed earlier in the chapter.)

Probably the most common reason why synergy opportunities are hard to evaluate is intrinsic uncertainty. Benefits may be hard to pin down or to forecast; compromise costs may be difficult to quantify, and may be seen differently by each unit; risks may loom larger or smaller depending on the circumstances of each unit. These uncertainties will make it difficult for different units to reach agreement on the likely net benefit – and disagreements at this level will almost certainly hinder progress, even if there is a large group benefit in the offing.

In the case of hard-to-evaluate opportunities, the role for the parent is to help with evaluations or impose its views. At Rentokil, for example, there are often judgements to be made about whether a marketing campaign that worked well in one branch, or business, or country will transplant well into other units. Differences in local circumstances have to be taken into account, so that plausible arguments both in favour of and against using the campaign elsewhere can be made. Where the units concerned cannot reach agreement, line managers in the parent, either at corporate, regional, divisional or area level, depending on the importance and scope of the issue, will arbitrate. These parent managers can reach a better-based assessment than the unit managers, because they are sufficiently close to each of the businesses to understand the detailed trade-offs, more aware of value that could accrue to the group as a whole, and in a better position to assess the level of risk that it makes sense for the group to run. In these circumstances, our general presumption that business unit managers will be better placed to evaluate opportunities

than parent managers is reversed, and the parent can add value by imposing its judgement about whether the linkage is worth pursuing.

Motivation opportunities

The next step in exploiting synergies depends on the motivation of the
participants. Even if they have seen links that offer potential advantages,
are they motivated to act on them? Lack of enthusiasm by one or more of
the units can stop collaboration dead in its tracks.

Our basic premise is that self-interest will motivate business managers
to link with each other provided there are obvious benefits to go for.
Indeed, our normal advice to parent managers who find business managers resisting their intervention ideas is to think again about whether
they may be pursuing mirages. Nevertheless, self-interest and local business-unit concerns do sometimes get in the way of initiatives that would
have value for the corporation.

Exhibit 3.5 Motivation parenting opportunities.

Causes	Roles for parent
Lack of interest	Reduce inertia, parochialism, bias
Lack of local pay-off • win/lose trade-offs • misaligned incentives • collective benefits	Increase local pay-offs • redistribute rewards • adjust incentives and corporate culture • champion the initiative
Personal frictions • personality clashes • rivalries • mistrust	Improve co-operative attitudes • socialisation, corporate culture • adjust structures, incentives to reduce rivalries and mistrust • address friction points • new appointments

Disincentives to pursue linkages that have a clear pay-off for the group come in a number of forms. A common problem is that managers in one or more of the units see personal costs rather than benefits in proceeding: the size of their personal empires or bonuses, for example, may be adversely affected. Another recurrent issue is personal animosities that prevent individuals from working constructively together. Motivational blockages to working together are all too familiar – and their removal provides a further source of parenting opportunities. Typical causes of motivational problems are shown in Exhibit 3.5, together with possible roles for the parent.

We have already dealt with the first problem, lack of interest, in the section on perception opportunities. Since both causes and remedies are similar in the case of motivation and perception issues, we shall not dwell on them again here.

Lack of local pay-off

Even the most attractive collaborations do not always yield benefits for all the units and managers. Frequently, there are win/lose trade-offs, whereby one unit gains a great deal while another loses. It may be beneficial to centralise production in one factory that is shared between two businesses; but one of the units must shut its facility and transfer production to the other. For some managers this loss may outweigh any benefit they gain. Win/lose trade-offs take many forms, depending on the specifics of the case, but, where they lead to a lack of pay-off for local managers in one or more of the units, they can crucially undermine motivation to pursue the synergies.

Misaligned incentives give rise to a particular type of win/lose trade-off. Performance-measurement and reward systems in many companies focus heavily on business-specific results, with little or no regard for contributions managers have made to other units or the group as a whole. Why should a manager risk damaging the performance of his or her own unit, with consequences for personal rewards and punishments, when there is no personal upside in helping the other unit? The incentives system determines the personal impact of cross-company collaborations, and all too often erects barriers that discourage managers from pursuing group benefits.

Linkages that collectively benefit the group but have modest upsides for each individual business can also create motivation problems. Is there a real pay-off for my business in adhering to new group policies on corporate identity? Or shouldn't I bother to change packaging or letter-heads that I am personally attached to? The upside for my unit may not seem great enough to make it worth the trouble – even though, from the group perspective, the pay-off across all the units is clear.

The parent has an important role to play in creating a better alignment between local and corporate interests. The national unit that loses out in a factory rationalisation can be offered added responsibilities for product development or marketing, or can be given lead manufacturing respon-sibility in another product range. ABB, for example, has carried through comprehensive reorganisation of its international production capacity, but win/lose issues have been mitigated by giving different countries the lead role in manufacturing different products. Few countries have lost out altogether.

The parent can also adjust performance measures and personal incen-tives so that they do not get in the way of valuable linkages. Transfer-pricing systems that allocate all the benefit from internal trading to one unit can be altered to reflect a more equitable division of profits; bonus formulas can be shifted away from exclusive focus on business unit results to incorporate corporate performance as well; personal as-sessments can be structured to place more emphasis on collaborative endeavours and good corporate citizenship. The increased emphasis that many companies have placed on personal responsibilities and individual business results during the last decade has often meant that incentives work against collaboration. Recognising the problem, companies such as ICI and BTR are now redesigning incentives with a less narrow busi-ness focus.

Incentive systems, however, cannot be sufficiently fine-tuned to pro-vide positive support for all valuable synergies. Adjusting managers' bonuses to reflect all their personal contributions to other units would cause daunting complexity, and there are some situations – for example, competition between businesses to become the lead unit for a product – where there may be no realistic way of compensating the loser. At best, major distortions and blockages can be eliminated. Beyond this, the role of the parent is to establish a culture of mutual support and sharing that encourages collaboration even where there is no direct pay-off for the individual. In some cases, the parent must be willing to impose decisions that are clearly beneficial for the group even though they damage some local unit interests.

Where the problem is that the businesses fail to see the pay-off of co-operating with group-wide policies and standards, the parent can forcefully champion the initiative. It can show the businesses why, for example, a common brand positioning and presentation across countries makes sense, bringing out the increasing importance of mobile consumers who travel between countries, or the dangers of arbitrage between countries that sell the same product at different prices. Perhaps most importantly, by making it clear that an initiative matters to the chief executive and the top team, the parent can show managers that there are likely to be negative personal repercussions for those that fail to support it.

Personal frictions

Whether because of personality clashes, fundamental differences in management style, deep-seated rivalry, or mistrust of hidden agendas, some managers find it almost impossible to work together. To take a common case, the regular evaporation of synergies foreseen in merger proposals is usually the result of managers from the two sides finding it impossible to work constructively with each other. This is not surprising. Managers from the different companies are likely to have grown up with different traditions and to harbour fears for the personal consequences of the merger. Moreover, they may have spent years rubbishing the approach of their opposite numbers, with whom they previously competed fiercely. To expect enlightened self-interest to overcome these frictions is unrealistic.

The role for the parent in overcoming personal frictions is clearly to take measures that improve co-operative attitudes. Some of these measures may concern the corporate culture. For example, Shell has always invested heavily in promulgating shared values and in human resource policies that promote them. The purpose is to socialise managers to work well with each other for the common good of the company, and to remove managers who are isolationist or unco-operative.

Personal rivalries may be unintentionally heightened by structures and incentives set up by the parent. If, for example, a company encourages three or four sector heads to compete for succession to the chief executive's chair, it must expect a certain rivalry between the contenders and mistrust of each others' intentions as they jockey for position. As a parent manager, take care not to promote frictions that clog the wheels of linkages that you are simultaneously trying to encourage.

Background measures, however, will not be sufficient to cope with open warfare. In this case corporate managers have no choice but to bang heads together. Ultimately, they may have to make new appointments. In one group, the CEO tried for five years to get the managers responsible for North American and European operations to co-operate. North America was run by an aggressive woman, with a strong commitment to militant feminist causes and a belief in an open management style. Europe was run by a laid-back and traditional Englishman, who preferred to operate through more formal hierarchical structures. Both managers privately aspired to run the global business that they expected might be set up, but meanwhile argued that there were few overlaps between their businesses that would merit collaboration. After a series of failed attempts to get the businesses to work together, each leading to bitter rows and recriminations, the CEO finally lost patience and fired both managers. In their place he appointed new people who are working well together on a range of sharing opportunities that had previously been impossible to progress.

Implementation opportunities

Even if the businesses have perceived the synergy opportunity, evaluated it correctly and are motivated to pursue it, there is still a final hurdle to cross: will they be able to implement the measures to exploit it? Do the businesses have the right skills and processes? Will the costs of implementation provoke second thoughts? Will the businesses find it easy to achieve their aims without parental help? Skill or process shortfalls can hamper implementation, and can therefore create a role for the parent. Exhibit 6 summarises why implementation opportunities arise and the associated roles for the parent.

Exhibit 3.6   Implementation parenting opportunities.

Causes	Roles for parent
Lack of skills or processes	Close the skills gap • coaching • help Establish suitable processes
Wrong attitudes	Shift attitudes • culture change • people change
Costs of implementation	Mitigate costs of implementation • economies of scale • funding for businesses
Hard-to-implement opportunities • multilateral • special skills needed • speed vital	Take the lead • co-ordinate, facilitate links • provide expertise • set the pace

Lack of skills or processes

Many linkage efforts require skilled managers to make them effective. For example, the business heads of a European speciality chemical company agreed that it would be valuable to combine resources to set up an Asia-Pacific representative office in Singapore. The aim was to improve sales effectiveness in markets that were unfamiliar to all the businesses. The initiative at first failed, because none of the businesses had a suitable candidate to head the Asia-Pacific office: the individual appointed was not well-connected in the region and lacked the skills needed to open up new accounts. A parent that could have provided a suitable manager from its central staff, or at least trained and coached the man appointed, would have greatly increased the chances of synergy being realised.

In many situations, particularly in the case of shared know-how, the potential benefits of collaboration hang on the existence of highly motivated individuals with outstanding skills. In principle, the units may agree that it makes sense to share marketing ideas; but if no unit has an expert candidate to take the job on, or if the candidate is unable to communicate his expert ideas, not much value is likely to be created. For improvements to be achieved, there must to be champions with the right skill levels. Where there are none in the units, the parent must help out by creating a centre of expertise.

Similarly, the barrier to making a linkage work may be the absence of a suitable process through which the interested parties can work together. In theory, units that want to co-ordinate their product offering should be able to set up a mechanism for bringing it about. In practice, the lack of established procedures may make it too hard. If parent managers see the lack of processes as a barrier, they can intervene to solve the problem.

Wrong attitudes

Implementation will only proceed smoothly if managers in all the business units support it. In part, this is a matter of local motivation, which we discussed in the previous section. However, there are also broader attitudinal issues. Is there a culture of co-operation in the group, or a climate of suspicion and competition? Are the units willing to accept and support corporate initiatives, or is there prevailing cynicism or a lack of discipline in carrying out corporate policies or instructions? Are the units willing to recognise when they need help from others, or do they prefer to plough their own furrows, come what may? The wrong basic attitudes make implementation of synergy measures much harder.

While it is not easy to get to grips with deep-seated attitudinal problems, the parent should not allow unco-operativeness, mistrust or indiscipline to go unchecked. By emphasising, reinforcing and rewarding certain behaviours, corporate managers can often gradually shift the culture. Or, if unit managers dig their heels in too far, management changes in the businesses may be necessary. Getting the corporate culture right is a vital component of synergy management, as we shall emphasise again in Chapter 4.

Costs of implementation

In sizing the prize, the businesses will have estimated the costs of putting an initiative into practice. How much time will be involved in cross-business meetings? What will it cost to develop joint promotional materials? How much of the R & D budget will have to be allocated to a combined product-development programme? Initial enthusiasm for synergy ideas often cools when the cost of pursuing them becomes clear. From the perspective of the businesses, a decision not to proceed may be the right one.

The parent, however, may be able to mitigate these costs. It can take advantage of economies of scale, for example by recruiting an IT professional to provide a central IT resource. In addition, the parent can relieve the businesses of bureaucratic constraints that add unnecessary costs – for example, a requirement to document and report to the centre all shared software or system developments. In these ways, the parent can tilt the cost-benefit balance back in favour of proceeding with the linkage.

A particular practical problem concerns the impact of the corporate budget process. Businesses are often inhibited from pursuing an attractive synergy opportunity because of short-term budget pressures. While they can see the benefits of global co-ordination of product development and launch plans, the costs in the current budget year would be high. The fact that some or all of the businesses would fail to hit their budget targets would be enough to deter many businesses from proceeding. In these circumstances, the parent can either realign performance measures and incentives or provide special funding to support the initiative. From a corporate perspective, this is admittedly 'funny money', but it may be necessary to persuade the businesses to go ahead with an initiative that has a long term pay-off.

Hard-to-implement opportunities

Just as some opportunities are intrinsically hard to perceive or evaluate, others are intrinsically hard to implement. It is never easy to effect co-operation between a large number of independent entities: multilateral networking is always much harder than where only two or three units are involved. Some link-ups require specialist technical or marketing skills, which are always in short supply. Other synergies – for example a joint bid for newspaper, book and television rights on a 'hot' story – need to take place quickly or they will fail. In these cases, relying on spontaneous self-interest is a mistake. The businesses may recognise the opportunity, but will probably each put it into the 'too difficult' box: none of them will have enough interest or clout to overcome the difficulties. The parent's role is then to provide the leadership to crack the difficulties, bringing together the interested businesses, providing specialist expertise, and generally pushing the joint effort forward.

Using parenting opportunities to shape interventions

The discipline of understanding the parenting opportunity helps managers avoid mirages and select suitable interventions.

Unless parent managers are sure that a parenting opportunity exists, our advice is not to intervene at all. Intervention where there is no real parenting opportunity is a prime cause of frustration, since the presumed benefit is likely to be a mirage. It is therefore vital to be as clear as possible about whether a genuine parenting opportunity exists.

But it is often hard to distinguish between mirage and reality. Is the failure of the businesses to work together the result of motivation problems or because the businesses have rightly assessed that opportunity costs are too high? Would a new corporate function provide just the help the businesses need to get an exchange of new product ideas going, or would it get in the way of beneficial sharing? We do not pretend that it is easy to judge whether a real parenting opportunity exists.

To test the reality of a proposed parenting opportunity, there are however two useful checks:

- Is there evidence from previous interventions that a parenting opportunity exists and that these interventions have yielded benefits? If we have a track record of success in pursuing parenting opportunities of this type, we can be more confident.
- Do the businesses concerned welcome the parent's involvement? If they do, we can be more certain that the opportunity is real.

If parent managers are still uncertain whether a parenting opportunity is real, they should proceed with caution. How to act in the face of this kind of uncertainty is discussed further in Chapter 6.

Correctly identifying a parenting opportunity is an important step towards choosing an intervention, since the role to be played by the parent follows from the cause of the parenting opportunity. If we decide that two businesses are not perceiving a benefit because they lack information about each others' sales activities, the parent's role is to improve the flow of information. If, however, the failure to work together stems from performance measures that emphasise each business's separate sales figures and fail to give credit for shared customers, the parent's role is to devise new incentive schemes that foster more co-operation. Thinking through the nature of the parenting opportunity, and hence the role that the parent needs to play, narrows the range of intervention options to be

considered. If the problem is one of information availability, it's no use
fine-tuning the incentive system. Conversely, if the businesses are not
working together because bonus schemes give no credit for joint sales,
circulating full sales visit reports will probably do more harm than good.
Interventions must fulfil the role that the parent needs to play.

By no means all parenting opportunities require intrusive interventions. Often, the role of the parent is to help the businesses improve
their own decision-making or to foster networking between them – for
example, by improving information flows, realigning incentives, or encouraging face-to-face contacts. In such cases, the businesses remain
ultimately responsible for decisions about whether and how to link with
each other, and the parent concentrates on removing the blockages that
may be preventing the businesses from recognising or acting on the benefits available. The advantage of such interventions is that final judgements
about the balance of costs and benefits remain with the business managers, who should usually be best placed to calculate the trade-offs.

There are some parenting opportunities, however, where the parent
needs to mandate a policy or decision and demand that the businesses
implement it. If, for example, the opportunity concerns standardising
brand presentations throughout the world, a networking approach that
leaves each business free to make its own decisions is unlikely to succeed. As we have argued, opportunities of this kind involve significant
collective, cumulative benefits, and need compliance from all units. On
the other hand, they are unlikely to be important enough to any one
unit to motivate it to lead the charge. To realise the opportunity, the
parent will have to take the initiative. It will need to formulate some
brand presentation policies that are then mandated for all units to follow.

Our discussion of the different sorts of parenting opportunities has
identified a number of roles for the parent that are likely to require
mandated decisions. These are summarised in Exhibit 3.7. In each case,
the nature of the parenting opportunity dictates a decisive intervention,
without which the opportunity is unlikely to be exploited. Even if the
corporate parent is a strong believer in decentralisation, it will have to
impose a decision if it wishes to grasp parenting opportunities of this
sort.

Exhibit 3.7   Roles for the parent that are likely to involve mandated decisions by the parent.

Role	Mandated decision
• Reducing deeply embedded inertia, bias, parochialism, personal friction, mistrust	• New appointments, new structures
• Promoting benefits that are collectively significant, but small for each unit and require 100% compliance (standardisation)	• Establish mandatory policies
• Championing radical new initiatives	• Take the initiative
• Rectifying deep seated bias in evaluation methods and processes, or shortcomings in implementation processes	• Mandate new methods and processes
• Pushing through initiatives with large but uncertain or risky net benefits	• Overrule unit opposition
• Pushing through win/lose initiatives when the loser cannot be adequately compensated	• Mandate the decision, or change the structure
• Setting the pace	• Require rapid implementation
• Changing attitudes	• Selective new appointments

The nature of the parenting opportunity also has implications for whether to use corporate staff. For many opportunities, line managers can do what is needed, for example by making suggestions to one unit about what it could learn from another. But there are opportunities where corporate staff have a vital role to play. For instance, experts with special technical skills may be necessary to evaluate and implement opportunities for sharing best practice in process engineering. If these skills are rare, it may be necessary for the parent to hire specialists and make them available to the businesses. In some situations, such as a central manufacturing services department, the skills needed will only be acquired through working with the range of businesses that the company has in its portfolio, which means that the parent will have to employ staff centrally in order for them to develop the relevant expertise. Exhibit 3.8 summarises roles for the parent that are likely to require use of parental staffs.

Exhibit 3.8   Roles for the parent that are likely to involve the use of parental staffs.

Role	Staffs needed
• Reduce scanning, evaluation or implementation costs	• Central staffs to exploit economies of scale
• Provide rare, specialist expertise in scanning, evaluation or implementation	• Relevant specialists
• Adjust local pay-offs in multilateral linkages to create net benefits for all/most units	• Central staffs to mitigate costs and leverage benefits
• Help with implementation	• Staffs with the necessary skills; financial (or other) resources as needed

Determining the nature of the parenting opportunity and the associated role for the parent therefore helps to establish what interventions are and are not likely to be effective. In the sidebar – 'Identifying parenting opportunities and intervention options' – we propose five questions that we have found helpful in the identification of parenting opportunities and intervention options, and show how these questions can be worked through for a company called Forestco.

Identifying parenting opportunities and intervention options

Understanding parenting opportunities requires a detailed analysis of the reasons why the business units are not taking full advantage of the synergy benefits on offer. It is based on this understanding that possible interventions options can be generated. Analysis of parenting opportunities is not easy. There are, however, certain questions that we have found to be useful prompts.

What if the businesses were independent?

Try to imagine a situation in which the businesses are not part of a single corporate entity. Would they now find it easier or more difficult to exploit the synergy opportunity? If it would be harder, and we can see why this is so, it may point to a role for the parent that should be reinforced. If, however, it might be easier, this may help us to see things that the parent is doing which are actually blocking beneficial linkages, and should be stopped.

The purpose of this question is to force a challenge to the existing parenting relationship. It is easy to take too much of this relationship as a given, and to deal only with incremental adjustments to it. By mentally stepping aside from the current ownership structure, it is often possible to open up thinking in productive ways.

Why intervene at all?

This question fundamentally challenges the presumption that the parent's natural job is to intervene. It takes us back to the basic assumption that, if there are benefits to be had, self-interest should usually lead to spontaneous decisions by the businesses to achieve them. Why, in this instance, do we believe that self-interest is not working?

By placing the burden of proof on the parent to justify an intervention, it forces explicit consideration of the nature of the parenting opportunity and the role for the parent. Exhibits 3.2–3.6 provide a checklist of parenting opportunities that might otherwise be missed. But a tough-minded and sceptical attitude should be taken to all proposed parenting opportunities. The purpose is not to find a plausible excuse for an intervention. It is to decide whether the centre has any business interfering at all.

Real opportunities or mirages?

There is almost always something that a parent can fasten on to that seems to offer the potential to increase synergy benefits, some parenting role that could conceivably add value. But are the benefits really substantial enough to justify the inevitable costs of the intervention? Have these costs received as much attention as the benefits? Is the net benefit big enough to warrant action?

Parents should concentrate their interventions on major opportunities rather than dissipate their efforts across many small initiatives. If the net benefit looks really worthwhile, go for it. But if it looks modest, hold back unless you are sure that the costs and downside risks are low.

What are rival parents doing?

This question is intended to open up thinking to options that may have been suppressed or omitted. Any company's corporate strategy and culture will influence its thinking about synergy opportunities, by emphasising (or de-emphasising) certain sorts of benefits or certain sorts of interventions. To the extent that other companies do not share these biases, their actions and interventions may reveal fresh opportunities.

Many companies are woefully ignorant of how their competitors manage cross-company links, and find it hard to make much progress with this question. However, with some systematic effort, it is not difficult to develop a profile of half-a-dozen interesting rivals, and our advice is that this investment in competitive intelligence – gathering is often very worthwhile.

Are the businesses supportive?

Our experience is that business managers are usually well placed to recognise the validity of parenting interventions. They will normally welcome interventions that are targeted on real parenting opportunities. If the businesses are supportive of the parent's interventions, this suggests that they will probably add value, and will certainly be easier to implement.

If the businesses are recalcitrant, the parent may paradoxically feel reinforced in its desire to intervene. 'Their opposition to the new policies just shows how strongly the NIH attitude has taken root, and how important it is to overrule it.' But we would advise caution. It may indeed show that there are attitudinal, personal or other blockages for the parent to overcome. But it is more often a sign that compromise costs, opportunity costs or other downsides are being underestimated by the parent. Take business resistance seriously. If an intervention does not receive business support, carefully re-examine the evidence in favour.

Vertical integration at Forestco

Forestco is an integrated forest-products company, with businesses in forestry, pulp, a variety of grades of paper, and some downstream activities such as carton manufacture. There is extensive internal trading between the upstream and downstream businesses, as well as open market, third-party sales. The supply relationship between the paper-making and carton-manufacturing businesses has often been fraught, but the corporate managers of Forestco believe that there should be valuable vertical integration synergies between the two businesses. They are keen to identify any parenting opportunities that they should pursue to increase the benefits from this linkage. How could our checklist of questions help?

What if the businesses were independent?

- They could, and probably would, enter into long-term supply agreements, with both sides negotiating to achieve (a) security of supply/offtake and (b) favourable prices. With a long-term contract in place, they would probably co-ordinate some but not all of their respective expansion plans. Currently, there are disputes about the internal transfer price and complaints about pressures on the downstream business to purchase internally.
- The parent needs to be clearer about what it wants to achieve through vertical integration that would not be achieved through third-party market relationships, and needs to find a new approach to transfer pricing and trading relationships that will cause less aggravation.

Why intervene at all?

- Previous frictions between the managements of the two businesses – partly caused by the trading rules imposed by the parent – mean that there is some mutual mistrust. Furthermore, the downstream carton business is not sympathetic to the importance of capacity utilisation in the upstream paper business.
- The parent may be able to intervene to improve relationships between the businesses. It should stop forcing the businesses to trade with each other, and recognise that they may have good commercial reasons for not wishing to do so. It should establish transfer prices that reflect, as far as possible, market prices. It may also be helpful to create more opportunities for the business managements to work together on other issues or to interact socially to allay mistrust. And the parent should consider what information or briefing it could provide to help both businesses to have a better appreciation of each other's critical success factors. This may help both businesses to see that a 'first refusal' right of supply for the upstream business, provided its prices and quality levels are competitive, would be valuable for the group, and that some collaboration on expansion plans could be useful

to allow the paper business to achieve better capacity utilisation.

Real opportunities or mirages?

- Forced internal supply at artificially high transfer prices may look like an attractive guaranteed route to market: but it is actually a mirage, since it simply represents cross-subsidy of the upstream by the downstream, and will result in the eventual failure of the downstream. First refusal rights of supply do have some benefits, depending on how much volume the downstream takes, but the level of benefits is probably fairly modest.
- The parent should be cautious in its interventions. There is a danger of chasing a mirage unless the parent has thought through exactly what it is trying to achieve, and it is not clear that there is a large opportunity to go for.

What are rival parents doing?

- There are several integrated competitors, some of which control internal cross supply tightly from the corporate centre. But there is no clear evidence that these competitors are outperforming more loosely integrated companies or companies that are not in the downstream businesses.
- The parent should not try to move far away from third party market relationships between the businesses

Are the businesses supportive?

- Past frictions have made the businesses suspicious of parental interventions. The downstream business, in particular, wants more commercial freedom to buy on the open market. There is, however, a basic recognition that both businesses are important to each other, and a desire for a better relationship.

- New initiatives by the parent that recognise and rectify past mistakes could be welcomed by the businesses.

Here are some intervention options that emerge from this assessment of the parenting opportunities:

- Scrap the old transfer pricing formula and either replace it with a formula based on specified third-party benchmarks or allow the businesses to negotiate freely without parental intervention.
- Stop forcing the businesses to trade with each other, but require the carton business to give the paper-making business first-refusal rights of supply at competitive prices: make clear that the parent will frown on failure to agree to do business together.
- Set up a joint project on future expansion plans (or possible acquisitions or ....) to engender better working relationships and/or hold periodic cross business meetings to discuss 'issues of common concern' and/or make some management changes to open up new personal relationships.
- Coach the business heads about the respective economics and CSFs of each other's businesses and/or encourage secondments at lower levels and/or provide more information to each business on the other's performance.

Summary

The mental discipline of pinpointing the parenting opportunity is probably the most valuable contribution that we have to offer to parent managers in search of synergy. It should help to offset both the synergy bias and the parenting presumption that so often result in the pursuit of mirages. It should also provide guidance on when and how the parent should intervene.

Analysis of parenting opportunities is not easy. We recognise that the parenting opportunity concept will be unfamiliar to many managers, and that it calls for a different mindset in thinking through synergy issues. To help in identifying parenting opportunities, we have therefore developed a comprehensive checklist of different categories. We have also discussed how to use the parenting opportunities thinking in devising intervention options. We believe that those who persevere in their efforts to pinpoint the parenting opportunity will be amply rewarded with better results from their synergy initiatives.

Understanding the parenting opportunity defines the role for the parent. But it seldom dictates a single preferred intervention option. There are usually different ways to intervene that could each achieve the desired end. To narrow the choice of intervention further, we also need to take account of the parent's skills and of knock-on effects, which are the subjects of the next two chapters.

4
Build on Parenting Skills

It requires skills to influence business unit managers to do something they are not choosing to do already. What is more, the parenting skills needed are different for different areas of synergy. Before choosing an intervention, parent managers need to judge whether they have or can build the skills to implement it.

In our experience the chances of success are low unless the company has either

- a well-grooved mechanism: an intervention that has been used successfully before to achieve similar kinds of synergy benefits; or
- a natural champion: an individual with the specialist knowledge, organisational respect, people skills, time and desire to make the intervention work.

Without a well-grooved mechanism or a natural champion, the chances of success are low.

Our third mental discipline is about implementation. Even if a synergy has been correctly sized and understood, parent managers still face a major task – choosing an intervention they are capable of implementing. Our advice is to choose interventions that build on skills the parent managers have or can develop. Too frequently managers are blinded by the 'skill presumption'. They presume they have the knowledge and skills needed to make their chosen intervention work. Surprisingly often they don't.

Parenting skills are not standard sets of competencies that result in good synergy management. They are idiosyncratic: they differ depending on the synergy being addressed and the intervention being used. The parenting skills needed to co-ordinate production planning are different from those needed to promote cross-selling. The parenting skills needed to run a co-ordination committee are different from those needed to design and police a transfer pricing system. The parenting skills needed to overcome entrenched resistance in one unit are different from those needed to help a unit with capability weaknesses. Before choosing an intervention, parent managers need to think carefully about whether they have what it will take to make the intervention work.

● A consumer-goods company wanted to co-ordinate manufacturing across two businesses in Europe. The businesses made similar, and in some cases identical, products. Parent managers felt there would be opportunities to share capacity, reduce transport costs, standardise ingredients and raise skill levels. They formed a committee consisting of the two manufacturing directors, chaired by the corporate technical manager, to oversee the effort.

Over a period of two years, the committee met every two months. It launched several projects. Staff assessed the efficiency of different plants; one product was moved to a factory in the other business to free capacity for a new product; and managers discussed production planning. But there were few major changes. Only small benefits were gained, and the costs of management and staff time may well have exceeded the benefits: the intervention failed.

In the third year, one of the managers on the committee retired, another moved to a different job. The remaining manufacturing manager took up dotted-line responsibility for the factories of both businesses. Within six months he had created large benefits from sharing capacity, reducing transport costs, standardising ingredients and sharing best practice. When asked why these changes did not happen before, the manager explained: 'Neither of the other two members of the committee were real manufacturing people. They just didn't know what was possible. As a result, every time I proposed a change, we had a project team analyse the pros and cons. To my colleagues, the risks and benefits seemed fairly well matched, so we didn't do anything. Once I had more influence, I was able to go for the benefits.'

This is a common story. New and complex link-ups need to be driven by someone who is intimately aware of the possibilities and has the particular skills to create the synergies: a person knowledgeable enough to lead the way and resourceful enough to win support from the doubters, cajole the organisation to adopt unfamiliar ways of working, empathise with winners and losers, and push ahead in the face of setbacks. We refer to these successful synergy-makers as 'natural champions': someone who has the skills to make the intervention work in this particular company.

These natural catalysts may not be needed if the company already has in place what we call 'well-grooved' mechanisms: familiar procedures which have been frequently and successfully used for handling similar types of collaboration issues. Most companies have some well-grooved mechanisms already in place. They may be transfer pricing systems for intertrading, project teams to handle co-ordination, policy committees for agreeing standards, central functions for defining best practice, and so on. Well-grooved mechanisms are part of a company's parenting skills. They represent established ways of working that have been used repeatedly and successfully in the past.

In this chapter we suggest that most successful synergy initiatives depend for implementation either on natural champions or on well-grooved mechanisms or on a combination of both. Without these parenting skills to build on, the chances of successful implementation are low.

Why implementation is an issue

Many promising synergy interventions fail. Parent managers do a good job of identifying a substantial benefit, understanding the parenting opportunity, and choosing a seemingly appropriate intervention. But they fall down on implementing it because they lack some vital skill or knowledge: they cannot make the co-ordinating processes work, or they lack the knowledge to persuade business managers to co-operate. As a senior manager in Unilever put it to us, 'Choosing interventions is only partly about costs and benefits. These do matter, but eventually it's about what makes the organisation sing.'

All interventions require skills on the part of the parent. The parent needs specialised knowledge of the particular synergy, the ability to make business managers pay attention and the processes and interpersonal skills to bring about the desired result. The idea of appointing a purchasing specialist to advise businesses on achieving benefits from pooled purchasing power may be excellent: but if the parent does not have the right person to do it, the new appointment will end up irritating and alienating the businesses. Alternatively, trying to achieve the same result through a wider sharing of purchasing information may, in theory, be sound: but if the outcome is simply indigestible mountains of paper which the businesses are unwilling or unable to wade through, the initiative will sink under its own weight. A lack of the right skills can thwart the best of intentions. Identifying the parenting opportunity is not sufficient. The parent must have the ability to act on it.

Another reason why implementation is an issue has to do with culture and context. Every organisation has a history which colours its assumptions, judgements and behaviours. These values, norms and rules of thumb are an important part of the context in which any intervention occurs. Seemingly obvious interventions that work well for one company may be wholly inappropriate for another. Parent managers need to pick the intervention that will work best in their context.

For example, suppose the aim of the intervention is to spread best practice in manufacturing, and the parenting opportunity is the chance to lower the cost to each unit of identifying and evaluating best practice. An obvious intervention might be to establish a manufacturing centre of excellence with the job of identifying and codifying world-class practice. But the obvious intervention may not fit the context. If the corporate culture contains a belief that business unit managers should have complete control over day-to-day operations, and there is a tradition of resisting standardised policies as intrusions on local autonomy, the attempt to impose best practice is likely to be resisted vigorously.

Maybe the answer is to make the adoption of best practice voluntary. However, if such an intervention reminds business unit managers of a similar attempt to establish environmental best practice standards which went disastrously wrong, the businesses may simply ignore the centre's efforts.

In these circumstances, a centrally led intervention will have low chances of success. The cultural norms and accumulated prejudices will make it hard for even the most skilled manufacturing expert to have an impact. The solution may be to involve a project team of business unit managers or some other more decentralised or bottom-up process.

A synergy effort that releases miraculous benefits in one organisation may fail dismally in another. This is why initiatives that seem – indeed are – straightforward in one setting may be fraught with difficulties in a different company. Parent managers therefore need to think deeply about implementation. What will be required to make this intervention work in our context? Are there other interventions that would reap most of the benefit with less risk of them going wrong? Do we have the skills needed to make this happen?

Assessing possible interventions

Parent managers in pursuit of a synergy opportunity must review their existing skills to determine whether they are adequate for the task. If they are not up to it, parent managers must consider whether and how new skills can be built. While these are not easy judgements to make, they merit careful attention.

Often, parent managers make these judgements in an intuitive, holistic fashion. 'I would feel a lot more comfortable asking our marketing director to lead this initiative than having it led by one of the business units,' the chief executive may say. Or 'I'm not sure that central packaging policies will work for us: why don't we get the business unit heads together to discuss it?' The basis for these views is a sense of what will and won't work, what will and won't make the organisation sing; and, in our experience, the intuitive judgements of parent managers about what will work are normally sound, provided that they give focused attention to the issue.

Sometimes, however, parent managers may find it more difficult to make the assessment. Sometimes an intervention is a new departure calling for untested skills. Another may involve untested people. The initiative may be a mixture of things that are likely to go well and other things that will be more problematic. Or, again, members of the top team may disagree about whether the intervention will be easy or difficult to carry through.

In these circumstances, a more systematic approach can be helpful. The solution is to make a detailed list of the things the parent managers are going to have to do.

Take the case of the consumer goods company wanting to co-ordinate manufacturing across two European businesses. What parenting skills will be needed to make the chosen intervention work (a committee of the corporate technical manager and the two manufacturing managers)?

The parent manager on the committee (the corporate technical manager) will find himself in one or more of the following situations:

- One manufacturing manager has made a proposal that the other does not accept. The parent manager generally supports the proposal.
- An agreed link-up is not being well implemented. The parent manager believes the reason is lack of commitment or skill on the part of one of the businesses.
- The parent manager has a hunch that greater co-ordination, for example production planning, would bring benefits, but both manufacturing managers are reluctant to discuss the subject.

If the committee is going to be an effective mechanism, the parent manager needs to be able to influence events. To do this he needs to have the staff support, access to the two businesses, and knowledge of manufacturing issues that enables him to check out whether his ideas are sound or not. He then needs the force of personality, respect from his colleagues and time to persuade the other managers to agree with him. Unless he has these skills and resources, his influence on the committee is likely to be minimal and the committee is unlikely to achieve much.

The skills and resources of the corporate technical manager are not however the only parenting skills needed to make this intervention a success. The CEO who sets-up the committee will need to be able to:

- Convince the manufacturing managers that the initiative is worthwhile and that the presence of the corporate technical manager will be useful.
- Judge what improvement objectives will be an appropriate target for the committee's work.
- Assess whether the committee is progressing well enough.

The full range of skills needed to make the co-ordination committee work is broad and complex. So how can parent managers understand the skills they need for an intervention and the likelihood of success?

Look at Exhibits 4.1 and 4.2, which address the European manufacturing example. Exhibit 4.1 deals with the original choice of intervention – the co-ordination committee – and clearly demonstrates that the probability of successful implementation in this case is low. The assessment is subjective, and the conclusions, both about what the key tasks are and about the skills needed for each, can be challenged. However, we have found that the process of formally laying out the tasks encourages more objectivity and helps to dampen the 'skill presumption'. Bias of some sort cannot be eliminated from qualitative judgements like these. Formal analysis is purely a way of exposing and disaggregating the judgements.

Another way of reducing the effects of the skill presumption is comparative analysis. By comparing one intervention against another, managers can decide which is more likely to succeed. Comparative analysis reduces

Exhibit 4.1

Implementation assessment		
Primary benefits:	Share capacity and standardise ingredients	
Parenting opportunity:	Rivalry between units and lack of attention to manufacturing linkages	
Intervention:	Manufacturing co-ordination committee	

Tasks	*Parenting skills needed*	*Comment/assessment*
1. Form committee with a positive attitude	• Ability to persuade members of the potential from linkages	• Low – one manufacturing director unconvinced of the potential
	• Ability to persuade members that this is the best intervention	• Medium – easy to get compliance, but harder to get commitment
	• Ability to gain agreement with members about the measures of success	• Low – parent managers not knowledgeable enough about co-ordinated manufacturing to define appropriate objectives
	• Ability to gain support from business managers to membership and role of parent manager	• Medium – business managers recognise the need for a third party, but unconvinced that technical manager is the ideal candidate
2. Make the committee work	• Parent manager has sufficient knowledge, staff or access to develop and confirm independent views	• Low – technical manager has limited manufacturing knowledge and limited access to staff or contacts outside the technical function
	• Parent manager has sufficient respect, force of character or authority to persuade others to support his views	• Medium – technical manager is highly respected but not very forceful
	• Parent manager has sufficient time, energy and commitment to get involved in issues	• Low – technical manager has no reduction in his other responsibilities
3. Monitor progress	• Define clear milestones	• Medium – primary benefits were clearly defined but parent managers did not have skill or confidence to quantify or qualify objectives. Technical manager did not have force of character to get committee to set own objectives. (No tradition of how to make these committees work)
	• Design process for reporting against the milestones and re-setting ambitions	• Low – no tradition of having such a committee report on its progress and re-set objectives. Managers assumed to be senior enough to decide for themselves

Exhibit 4.2

Implementation assessment

Primary Benefits: Share capacity and standardise ingredients
Parenting Opportunity: Rivalry between units and lack of attention to manufacturing linkages
Intervention: Give one manufacturing director responsibility for both manufacturing operations; place a more junior manager in charge of the 'second' business's manufacturing (choose a person acceptable to the lead manufacturing director); set up a dotted line responsibility between the junior manufacturing manager and the chief executive of the 'second' business.

Tasks	Parenting skills needed	Comment/assessment
1. Set up the change in organisation	• Ability to select the 'best' of the two manufacturing directors	• High – one was obviously more knowledgeable and committed to manufacturing
	• Ability to appoint an 'acceptable' junior manager in the 'other' business	• High – it happened that the right candidate was number two to the existing manufacturing director of that business. Moreover, the surplus manufacturing director had an alternative job to go to
	• Ability to make the dotted line relationship work	• Medium – little experience of this in the company. Lead manufacturing director a clear 'natural champion'. Chief executive and marketing manager of other business prepared to trust lead manufacturing director
	• Ability to gain agreement to measures of success	• Medium – parent managers not knowledgeable but able to set broad cost per ton objectives
2. Make the new responsibility work	• Lead manufacturing manager has sufficient knowledge, staff and access to develop and confirm his views	• High
	• Lead manufacturing manager has sufficient force of character and authority to persuade others	• High
	• Lead manufacturing manager has sufficient time, energy and commitment to get involved	• High, particularly because he re-organised to release two senior managers as project leaders

the temptation to argue that the parent is equally capable of implementing all initiatives. The process of capturing comparative judgements is explained further in Chapter 6.

Exhibit 4.2 looks at a second intervention – the decision to put one manufacturing director in charge of all the factories. The analysis shows that this intervention has a much higher chance of success. Even though the intervention is not a well-grooved mechanism, being the first of its kind, the manufacturing director is a natural champion of the initiative and the parenting skills needed to set the intervention up and support him are largely available.

Exhibits 4.1 and 4.2 are focused on the tasks that the CEO and the parent manager face and whether they have the skills and resources to execute them well. They do not address the second reason why implementation is hard: problems with the culture or context. If the culture in the company was alien to committees or to dotted line relationships this would have to be taken into account. If the manufacturing directors of the two businesses didn't like each other or were competing for a future promotion, this would have to be taken into account.

We have no clever way of analysing the culture or context issues to help managers; but we believe they need to be analysed. A list of culture and context pros and cons can be made for each intervention that is being considered. This will help parent managers think about what they will have to do to overcome the problem areas and whether they have the skills and resources to succeed.

The approach we suggest enables managers to go into as much detail as necessary to judge the implementation challenge of different interventions. Sometimes a judgement can be made without much analysis. In other cases a detailed analysis is helpful. The main concern in either case is to avoid the complacency of the skill presumption.

Well-grooved mechanisms

The easy answer to the implementation challenge is to choose well-grooved mechanisms: tried and tested procedures that have repeatedly proved their worth for similar purposes. Examples are the setting up of a 'working group' in Unilever, forming a 'task' or a 'project team' at Canon, producing a 'consultation document' at Shell, creating a 'central service' at Whitbread, or a 'suggestion' from one of the Mars brothers at Mars – all are well-grooved mechanisms for their own companies. The important corollary, of course, is that they would almost certainly work far less well, or not work at all, in other companies.

● At Canon for example, there are five different mechanisms for co-ordinating product development – Working Groups, Groups, Task Forces, Tasks, and Major Project Teams. Initial exploration of an area of common product or market interest would be through a Working Group. The Working Group is a temporary mechanism involving part-time managers from different businesses and central functions. A Working Group is normally small: just a handful of managers are involved. At the other end of the scale is a Major Project Team. These are only created once Canon has decided to launch a new product initiative in a market or technology not already covered by one of the businesses. Major Project Teams are permanent structures (at least until they are converted into new business units) and involve full-time membership from hundreds of managers from different businesses and central functions.

   Canon has taken hundreds of product ideas through the Working Group stage and runs a handful of Major Project Teams each year. The mechanisms have been well bedded in and managers assigned to a Working Group or a Major Project Team know what to expect. Canon also has an organisation structure that supports these mechanisms. There are large central functions with the ability to place 10 or even 100 staff on a Major Project Team. There is continuous movement between central staff and the businesses making it possible for the central staff to replenish their numbers and making it easier for business units to second managers onto projects.

   The results of Canon's process are also remarkable. The company has successfully entered a number of new fields with radical products and business positionings. The successful Major Project Team eventually becomes a new business and another engine for Canon's growth.

● At Whitbread, a British beer and restaurant company, a well-grooved mechanism is the creation of a central function with service contracts with the businesses. The purpose of the central function is to build expertise, encourage best practice sharing and gain economies of scale. The purpose of the service contract is to retain as much influence with the business units as possible. Often staff from the central function are located in the business units to ensure they are sensitive to the business's needs.

Whitbread's well-grooved mechanism has been used in property management, supply chain management, central purchasing and central product development. It is supported by a fundamentally co-operative culture where stories of what happened to those who had an isolationist mentality are told with relish.

It is a mechanism that has evolved. Not all of Whitbread's central functions have been wholly successful. There have been periods of too much centralisation and too much bureaucracy. But the outcome has been the development of a mechanism for gaining the benefits of centralised services that works in the Whitbread context.

The advantages of a well-grooved mechanism are self-evident. It has all been done before. Parent managers know what influence is likely to be needed. They have honed the skills that will be called on. They can anticipate how the organisation will react. They can tell who the winners and losers will be and how to balance the effects. With a well-grooved mechanism, parent managers can be confident that implementation issues will not be a problem.

Similarly, well-grooved mechanisms are also easier for business unit managers to work with, since they know what to expect. Because they know how to make the intervention work for them, they can help it work for the organisation as a whole.

Companies develop well-grooved mechanisms for a wide variety of collaborative tasks. In our research, we were initially struck by the frequent lack of alignment between types of benefit and the implementation methods chosen. For example, three companies, faced with the challenge of co-ordinating pricing across Europe in the face of cross-border retailers, each chose a different way of proceeding. We were also struck by the fact that some companies in the research appeared to find a particular mechanism easy to execute, while others found it horribly difficult.

The explanation behind both of these research-based observations is well-grooved mechanisms. Different companies choose different interventions partly because they have different well-grooved mechanisms. Moreover, companies that find certain linkages 'horribly difficult' either have no well-grooved mechanisms or none that are suited to the task.

We shall say more about well-grooved mechanisms in Chapter 7, which describes a method for reviewing a company's overall approach to synergy linkages, including an assessment of its well-grooved mechanisms. The question facing a parent manager with a specific decision to make, however, is when to rely on a well-grooved mechanism and when not to?.

Our advice is straightforward. If in doubt, use a well-grooved mechanism, even if it does not seem an ideal match for the parenting opportunity. So long as it is likely to release at least 70 or 80 per cent of the benefit, it will probably be more effective than choosing a new intervention that both parent and business managers are unfamiliar with.

There are two situations where a well-grooved mechanism is not appropriate. The first is where the parent manager wants to use an intervention as the initial or reinforcing step in creating a new well-grooved mechanism.

● For example, after the privatisation of Regional Electricity Companies (RECs) in Britain in 1989, many set up separate business units for different activities within the company. A network business focused on managing the distribution grid. An engineering business focused on doing repair and new building work. A supply business focused on selling electricity and providing support and billing services.

   Previously, issues that cut across the different activities were handled by line management processes, central policies and technical relationships between middle managers. The well-grooved mechanism was to discuss the issue at middle-level and, if agreement on action could not be reached, bring it to the attention of the next management layer.

While some RECs continued to use their established mechanisms in the new context, others set about creating new mechanisms that would make it easier to reduce the management hierarchy and eliminate cumbersome central policies. A common choice was to establish 'service contracting'. With this mechanism, service contracts were written to cover the supply of services, information or products from one business unit to another. The service contracts were negotiated between the businesses, subject to arbitration by senior management. Initially, the businesses did not have good negotiating skills, and senior management was often heavy-handed in its arbitration. As a result, some inappropriate contracts were signed. However, as managers gained more experience and the contracts grew in comprehensiveness and authority, they became well-grooved mechanisms for dealing with many complex relationships between business units.

The second reason for not choosing a well-grooved mechanism is when the parent manager is convinced that the mechanism is not up to the job.

● One service company with two main lines of business had traditionally kept the operations separate, handling co-ordination issues between them at arms length. The company was a partnership, and the culture encouraged networking, respect and co-operation between the partners. This meant that an arms-length, mutual-benefits approach to handling synergies worked well.

Problems arose, however, when the two businesses began to expand in Asia. Because the markets were different, the traditional boundaries around the segments served by each business became blurred. As a result, the businesses found themselves in conflict over clients and market positioning. An arms-length, mutual-benefits approach could not resolve the conflicts: it led to the businesses deciding to compete rather than co-operate.

The parent manager, in this case the senior partner, realised that a new mechanism was called for. He needed to find a new way of dealing with conflicts of this nature. After experimenting with alternatives, he found that the most effective mechanism was to create a unified business in Asia that was jointly owned by the two businesses. The company had no previous experience of handling internal joint ventures; clearly, it was an unfamiliar intervention. However, it was effectively championed by the senior partner. He carefully chose someone to run the joint venture who had had experience working in both businesses, and he actively intervened whenever tensions between the businesses began to rise.

Using a new mechanism creates fewer problems if parent managers already have most of the skills needed to make it work. Skills assessment is therefore particularly important if a decision not to use a well-grooved mechanism is being contemplated. If the skills are in place, there should be few implementation problems. If they are not, an active and talented natural champion will be needed to create the change needed.

Before we close our discussion of well-grooved mechanisms, a word of caution is in order. Well-grooved mechanisms are sometimes overused. Because they are easy to implement, and cause little friction, they are brought into operation even when they are unsuited to the parenting opportunity. For example, a company that successfully handled joint branding, advertising and packaging issues through a marketing co-ordination committee, tried to use the committee to develop a new corporate logo. Although the committee eventually succeeded, a centrally directed process would have been much more efficient. In another company, task forces are the normal mechanism for handling cross-unit marketing issues. Therefore, when the company wanted to share information on pricing policies, its automatic reaction was to set up a task force. Information was in the end shared, but a technology-based solution – i.e. using Lotus Notes – would have been much more efficient than the task force. Well-grooved mechanisms can also be overused in pursuit of small (or non-existent) benefits, or for excessive exploration of uncertain benefits (see Chapter 6).

Inappropriate use of well-grooved mechanisms can undermine their value to the organisation. If managers are frequently involved in a mechanism that doesn't deliver, they quickly lose interest and confidence. The best well-grooved mechanism is one that is used regularly but sparingly, and only for initiatives with a big pay-off. The efforts won't always be successful, but they must always be visibly worthwhile. Managers must associate the mechanism with initiatives that merit their support and energy.

Natural champions and new parenting skills

Opportunities that cannot be addressed by well-grooved mechanisms entail new ways of working for both parent and business-unit managers. As all those who have tried to manage change know, new ways of working or new organisational skills are hard to develop without an individual or group of individuals championing it and making it happen.

It is worth understanding this point more fully. Why is it hard to put into action a synergy intervention that is not well-grooved? First, there are embedded commitments to existing behaviours and organisational routines. Second, in most organisations there is little or no slack, a new intervention requires managers to reset their priorities and loads new items on to an already full agenda. Third, new interventions require new ways of working, new skills and new working relationships. These take time to build. Fourth, things get worse before they get better. This is Murphy's Law of Change. Change nearly always involves a step back before forward motion is resumed. Fifth, most interventions involve shifts of power between businesses or from businesses to parent. Skilful advocacy and/or forceful persuasion are needed to overcome the resistance that these shifts create.

Creating new mechanisms and building new parenting skills is never easy. Managers must be 'unfrozen' from attachment to old ways of working, and a change programme pursued, often over an extended period of time. Our research shows that the chances of success are low unless efforts are led by 'natural champions'.

So what is a natural champion? Natural champions are intimately acquainted with the details of the situation. They know the range of possibilities, understand the pros and cons of competing priorities, are aware of the mental maps of the managers, and grasp the win/lose issues. At the same time, they must be respected by the managers involved.

They must also be committed to completing the task and willing to devote the time and energy necessary to turn the potential into reality.

A natural champion does not have to be a parent manager. Often the natural champion is one of the business unit managers.

● In one consumer product company an effort to define best practice in market research techniques was led by the market research manager of one of the business units. The company had formed a committee to 'harmonise market research techniques across Europe'. The objective was to make comparison across countries possible.

The market research manager of the UK, who was on the committee, had been involved in a previous exercise in another division of the company. This exercise had got bogged down over disagreements about standards. The UK market research manager therefore persuaded the other members of the committee to focus initially on best practice rather than standardisation.

A project, led by the UK market research manager, was launched to review the literature on the subject and develop an intellectual structure for defining best practice. This structure was then used to develop principles and policies which were sold to the country-based, market research managers on the logic of quality rather than standardisation.

'In the other division everybody reacted to being told what to do and how to do their research. We found it much easier to persuade people if we used the best practice logic. We have tried to impose guidelines, but we have not just told managers to use a particular technique without explaining why we thought it was the best available.'

The UK market research manager was a clear champion of this unusually successful project. He had the technical skills to know what to do, the respect of his colleagues to gain their support and the understanding of how local managers would react.

The natural champion in some cases may not even be part of the organisation. Companies frequently use consultants as natural champions of new internal initiatives.

● One bank recognised that it was falling behind competitors in developing relationship management systems for its large corporate customers. Corporate customers purchased products from most of the bank's business units. Relationship management systems, which co-ordinated the serving of these customers, were believed to improve both service quality and profitability.

The problem the bank faced however was a lack of experience. None of the relevant corporate or international bankers had had relationship management experience and rivalry between the domestic and international business units was making spontaneous collaboration unsuccessful.

The chief executive therefore chose an outside consultant, with broad experience of implementing relationship management systems to help. The chief executive was careful to ensure the consultant would stay with the project for at least a year. He also took time to introduce the consultant to the businesses gently. He wanted the businesses each to have a relationship with the consultant before the project started. Over the ensuing nine months the consultant developed the information systems needed, demonstrated the profit potential of relationship management, led a pilot project with 10 major customers and convinced both sets of managers that their current way of operating was behind best practice. At the end of nine months the chief executive was able to restructure with little resistance from the two businesses. He created a corporate banking unit by combining elements of the domestic and international banks.

If a natural champion is not available it is often better to do nothing. Launching a new intervention without a champion dedicated to seeing it through is dangerous. Not only is there a high risk of the intervention failing or producing only limited results; it may sour the atmosphere for future attempts to make the linkage work, or make managers wary of future attempts to use a similar intervention for other purposes. Unless the probability of success is high, our advice is drop it.

Summary

In this chapter we emphasised the importance of our third mental discipline – build on parenting skills. Do the parent managers have the capability to implement the chosen intervention?

We have observed that parent managers often presume they have the skills to intervene in the way they want to. Our third mental discipline is an antidote to this skill presumption.

A detailed assessment of the implementation tasks and the skills needed to carry out each task is the obvious solution to the skill presumption. But it requires demanding analysis and runs the danger of creating analytical paralysis. By thinking in terms of well-grooved mechanisms and natural champions, it is often possible to make as good a judgement without the detailed analysis.

If an intervention is familiar and has been used repeatedly for similar synergy purposes, the chances of success are high. If, on the other hand, the intervention is unfamiliar, requiring new behaviours and skills that clash with the prevailing culture, beware: the chances of success are low. New or unfamiliar interventions are best avoided unless they are led by a champion who has the skills, energy and support to make them work.

Yet every well-grooved mechanism was unfamiliar at one point. Parent managers also need to think about the dynamics of their organisational capability. Today's linkage issues may be the opportunity to start creating a well-grooved mechanism that will pay dividends tomorrow. Sometimes parent managers need to push ahead with unfamiliar mechanisms that are not led by natural champions. Since these interventions are likely to absorb particularly large amounts of management time and face many false starts, parent managers need to limit their number and be confident that the longer term prize – the creation of a new well-grooved mechanism – will be worth the effort.

5
Look for Downsides

Downsides and upsides can occur in four areas:

- *Business mindsets:* the commercial strategies and rules of thumb that managers use to run their businesses. Links between business units can improve or contaminate current mindsets.
- *Organisational dynamics:* the direction of change in the culture and way the organisation works. Linkage interventions can support or hinder the changes that are underway.
- *Other parenting influences:* the impact parent managers are trying to have in other areas such as performance management. Interventions can facilitate or disrupt the other influences the parent is trying to have.
- *Motivation/innovation:* the energy in the organisation and the commitment to creativity and invention. Links can reduce or enhance feelings of ownership, team working and competitiveness which are often critical to motivation and innovation.

Parent managers particularly need to look out for downsides because of the mental bias in favour of upside thinking.

We pointed out in Chapter 1 that 'insufficient attention to downsides' is a regular cause of frustration in synergy management. Our last mental discipline addresses this difficulty. Parent managers should ask themselves: 'If we carry out this intervention, what will be the effect on the broader relationship between the parent and the businesses, on how managers in the businesses think and feel, and on the dynamic of the organisation?' We are particularly concerned about four kinds of negative effect: contaminating the thinking of some business managers; creating resistance to broader organisational changes; sapping initiative and motivation; and reducing the effectiveness of the other influences of the parent.

We are concerned about downsides because we observe that parent managers often give them too little attention. But knock-on effects can also be highly positive. A successful collaboration can enhance the effectiveness of other parenting influences. It can add momentum to organisational change. It can reinforce motivation, encourage innovation and improve the quality of the thinking in some businesses. Take time and care, then, to assess the likely positive and negative consequences of an intervention.

Managers normally make an assessment of knock-on effects intuitively. They comment:

- 'This will confuse the organisation. It will give the wrong signals. We need a way of getting at this that supports our other initiatives.'
- 'There is a danger that the initiative will interfere with our normal control and accountability process. We need to carry it through without putting at risk our current system.'
- 'This should be a big boost for motivation. It will reinforce the team spirit and energy we have in the current set-up.'
- 'An added benefit is that business A will influence the other businesses. By mixing the managers together, they will see the success of A's strategy and culture and will want to emulate it.'

These intuitive judgements are on the mark: knock-on effects can only be assessed qualitatively as potential risks and opportunities. In this chapter, we are not trying to offer structured analytical tools for quantifying knock-on effects. We are more interested in encouraging a mental discipline. We want parent managers to think about both positive and negative effects in four different areas – impact on business mindsets, impact on organisational dynamics, impact on other parenting influences, and impact on motivation and innovation.

In each case, our conclusion hardly needs stating: choose interventions that are likely to have positive knock-on effects and avoid those with a high risk of negative consequences. However, we urge managers to concentrate particularly on negative effects; from experience we know that insufficient attention to downsides is a frequent source of unpleasant surprises.

Business mindsets

Part of the capabilities of any manager or organisation are the unspoken thought-structures that frame business judgements: who to put in which job, what strategies to prioritise, what price to put on a new product, what level of maintenance to apply to an ageing machine, and innumerable other day-to-day decisions. These mental frameworks are a combination of commercial know-how, rules of thumb, management philosophy, attitudes, culture and other ways of thinking. We refer to them as 'business mindsets', and what is important is that they differ from one business to another. The business mindset of a restaurateur is different from that of a computer system specialist, which differs again from that of an oil magnate or pharmaceutical manager.

The knock-on issue centres on the impact an intervention will have on business mindsets, and the effect a change in mindset will have on the decisions managers make. When two businesses work together to develop a synergy opportunity, they influence each other's mindsets. Likewise when businesses become involved with parent managers. If the influence is positive, there is fusion or synthesis: the blending of ideas improves the mix. If the influence is negative, the effect is contamination: the blend is confusing or diffuses the rigour of the original thinking.

Since parent managers are in the business of influencing the thinking and behaviour of business managers, we might suppose that they would be particularly alert to the impact of their interventions on mindsets – and at one level they are, as the quotes on page 119 testify.

The problem is not a lack of attention to mindsets but rather a lack of awareness of the dangers. Parent managers are readily inclined to see the potential upside of bringing managers from different businesses together. But in their enthusiasm they rarely think much about the potential downside and, even if they do, they underestimate its possible extent. This is the 'lack of attention to downsides' bias.

● One example illustrates this well. A diversified retailer with businesses in appliance retailing, Do-it-Yourself (DIY), supermarkets, and books had recently bought an appliance retailer in another country. One reason for the acquisition was to explore the potential for developing an international appliance-retailing network which could benefit from combined purchasing (the appliance industry is increasingly dominated by a few global suppliers such as Matsushita and Electrolux) and from shared know-how.

The group CEO decided to pursue the opportunity by putting the chairman of the existing appliance-retailing business in charge of both operations. Since the newly acquired business was significantly less profitable, the assumption was that it would quickly absorb the lessons of the success of its sister company.

Managers focused initially on the potential for purchasing synergies. Some small synergies were quickly realised, but large synergies appeared less obvious because the two businesses were buying surprisingly different ranges of products, with different proportions of retailer-branded product and a wide spectrum of price points.

As the two management teams explored the potential, they concluded that big savings could only be achieved if the two businesses bought identical products. Initially this solution did not find favour. However, as the less profitable business learnt more about the purchasing strategies and pricing of its more successful partner, the thinking began to change.

The more profitable business sold on quality and service, attracting a segment of customers who were not driven primarily by price. The less profitable business had succeeded originally by undercutting its competitors; it still operated a pile-it-high, sell-it-cheap regime. Attracted by the success of the quality business, however, and keen to develop buying synergies, managers in the less profitable retailer began to change course. They bought some better-quality product, improved service levels and raised prices.

The result was disastrous. The company's traditional customers went elsewhere for their bargains, while upmarket purchasers stuck with their traditional suppliers. The strategic error was spotted and reversed, but it took more than a year to remove the inappropriate product from the supply chain, and the company suffered trading losses and major write-offs. The lure of synergy in this case contaminated the thinking of the managers in the less profitable business.

Exhibit 5.1   Conditions where contamination risks are high

Fundamental condition

The businesses are different in ways that require managers to have different mindsets:

- different critical success factors

Magnifying conditions

- Important differences between the businesses are 'subtle'
- Some businesses feel pressure to emulate other units
- Managers will be transferred between the businesses
- Parent managers do not have a good 'feel' for the businesses

---

To inoculate themselves against this danger, parent managers should be aware that contamination of this sort is always a risk when certain conditions prevail (Exhibit 5.1). Contamination problems occur when critical success factors (CSFs) in the business units differ, and hence call for different business mindsets. If the success factors are the same, there is no reason for the mindsets to be different and no danger of contamination. If the success factors differ, as between pile-it-high and quality retailing, the mindsets need to be different too. In that case contamination is a possibility.

We have tried to develop a precise tool for diagnosing differences in success factors between businesses – and failed. At one level of analysis, all businesses differ in some degree. At another level, all businesses are the same, requiring 'good management' to be successful. Meaningful judgement lies somewhere between these two extremes. Every Macdonald's franchise is different from every other, but there are more similarities than differences, and the differences are in areas less critical to success. Pile-it-high retailing has similarities with quality retailing, but there are more differences than similarities and the differences are in areas critical to success. For parent managers therefore the issue is one of studying differences and similarities and deciding which are important to success.

If the fundamental condition exists – important differences between the businesses – there is a risk of contamination. How big? There are four amplifying conditions that can magnify or diminish the risk.

1   How subtle are the differences between the businesses? If the important differences are obvious, as between hamburger restaurants and pharmaceuticals, the risk of contamination is low. There is little chance of a restaurant manager being unduly influenced by the mindset of a pharmaceutical manager or vice versa. Where the important differences are more subtle, as between, say, hamburger restaurants and pizza restaurants, or between a European perfume company and one in Latin America, it is much easier to get the mindsets confused. For example, a common mistake made by

companies expanding internationally is to apply a successful domestic formula to operations in other countries, where the differences
are not obvious or well understood.

2   How much pressure do the businesses feel to emulate other units?
Many synergy situations involve businesses of unequal status. One
of the businesses is larger, more profitable, more obviously part of
the core than others. In these circumstances, the lower status business is more likely to be influenced by the higher-status operation
than vice versa. This is what happened in the appliance-retailing
case. To some degree, this form of contamination happens whenever businesses are brought together in a portfolio – lower-status
businesses try to emulate higher-status ones in order to gain standing. The tendency is exacerbated by deliberate efforts to develop
synergies.

Sometimes the pressure for emulation is built into the intervention, as in the case of the appliance retailer. In these situations the
danger of contamination is greatly increased.

3   Will managers be transferred between the businesses? Interventions that swap managers between businesses increase the potential
for contamination. When managers move, mindsets move with
them. It is not uncommon for colleagues to comment that it took
six months or a year for an incoming manager to shake off the
ingrained attitudes and assumptions (i.e. mindsets) from his or her
previous job.

In some managerial functions this is less of a problem. Finance,
human resources and information systems managers find it easier to
move successfully between businesses, since their mindsets are con-
ditioned more by their functional discipline than by the characteristics
of the individual business. But in operating jobs, such as marketing, manufacturing or distribution, the managerial tasks and related
mindsets are often remarkably diverse.

The more senior the managers that move across, the greater the
danger that they will refuse to accept the mindsets of their new
colleagues and try to impose their own. In this case contamination
is a distinct possibility.

4   How good a 'feel' do parent managers have for the businesses? Where they understand the businesses well, particularly the differences between them, the likelihood of contamination is small. Parent managers will reinforce the differences where necessary and thus shield businesses from undue influences. The parent manager can point out subtle differences that need to be honoured, reduce the pressure on low-status or unselfconfident businesses to emulate their peers, and veto the transfer of inappropriate managers.

If, on the other hand, parent managers do not understand the businesses or the differences between them, they can unwittingly amplify the contamination risk. The parent manager can ignore subtle differences, create pressure to emulate inappropriate models, and transfer the wrong managers. Worse still, the parent manager who lacks feel can impose unsuitable policies and give poor guidance, thus becoming part of the contamination problem.

The implication of our observations on business mindsets is that parent managers should be aware of those situations where contamination risks are high. In those situations, they should design an intervention that minimises the danger, for example by:

- reinforcing the differences that need to be maintained;
- encouraging businesses to react like equals, not superiors and inferiors;
- limiting interaction unless it involves arm's length negotiations.

On the other hand, in situations where contamination risks are low, parent managers should be looking for interventions that promote synthesis rather than separation. Likely measures include:

- moving managers between the businesses;
- encouraging sharing and dialogue;
- favouring high-performing businesses with the highest status;
- urging common policies, practices and performance standards.

Mindset contamination is a particularly difficult knock-on effect to judge. When infection occurs, the costs are high, nearly always outweighing the linkage benefits. Our advice to parent managers is to assess the degree of risk from contamination using the criteria in Exhibit 5.1, and then, if the risk is high, to choose interventions that minimise the dangers.

Organisational dynamics

All organisations are in a constant process of change. Habits, values, attitudes, systems and structures are all on the move, each affecting and being affected by all the others.

External factors – changes in markets, the industry and technology – also feed into the process. For some organisations change is traumatic, for others it goes on almost unnoticed. Nevertheless, for all organisations it is possible to define a direction of movement. The company is decentralising or centralising. It is becoming more informal and open or more structured and hierarchical. It is becoming more customer oriented, more performance oriented, more technically oriented, more quality oriented or some other direction of change.

The knock-on issue is: does the proposed intervention go with or against the corporate grain? Will the intervention help or hinder the move to be more customer-oriented? Will it interfere with or support the internationalisation effort? Will it reinforce or confuse the decentralisation trend?

● A computer company faced the problem of co-ordinating product specifications across regional businesses. Each region wanted some different product specifications. If they all got what they wanted, proliferating product variations would create excessive costs. At the same time, a product that met all specifications would be too exclusive. Two interventions were being considered: a specifications committee led by the central technical vice president with participants from each region; or a transfer-pricing system that attempted to take account of the full cost implications of any variation from the basic model.

Most managers agreed that the co-ordination committee provided the best potential for optimising the number of variations. The technical VP was well regarded by the regional technical managers, and co-ordination committees of this kind were a fairly common mechanism in the company.

But the parent manager felt uneasy. The company had recently launched a campaign to raise profitability which involved more decentralisation, more accountability and tougher performance targets. A co-ordination committee would have been a good solution in the centralised culture of the past. But would it be right for the new performance-oriented culture she was trying to inculcate? In fact, choosing the more decentralised, less optimum intervention might be just the kind of signal the organisation needed to reinforce the new accountabilities. In other words, the knock-on effects on the organisational dynamic were an important criterion in this manager's thinking.

Parent managers are normally well attuned to the impact of such initiatives on organisational dynamics. They have an instinctive understanding of the direction the organisation is moving in and the likely positive or negative effects of a particular intervention. The thoughts of the parent manager in the computer business are not untypical. The mental discipline is therefore to check that this area of knock-on effect has been addressed; in particular that some creative energy has been put into identifying interventions that will reinforce rather than cut across the organisational dynamic.

There are three further points to make concerning organisational dynamics. The first point is to underline the value of developing new well-grooved mechanisms. An important knock-on effect can be the creation of and experimentation with a mechanism that may have much wider value to the organisation.

● For example, the corporate human-resources manager in one company wanted to improve co-ordination of management training. He could see potential benefits in a number of areas, including cost saving, quality improvements and network building. He favoured a management–

development steering group as an initial, mainly exploratory, mechanism. His boss, however, suggested he centralise part of the management–development function based on service contracts with each of the businesses.

The chief executive perceived a number of other areas where functional co-ordination benefits might be possible, while some of the existing central functions were coming under criticism from the businesses. He was therefore on the lookout for an opportunity to experiment with the service-contract mechanism, which he reasoned might provide a solution to many of his functional co-ordination needs. He wanted to try out a new intervention that could become a well-grooved mechanism for the future.

The second point draws on the example from the computer industry. It is about the 'signal' value of interventions. Managers read actions more closely than words. They draw messages from the decisions their superiors make – and they are not always the messages that are intended. Each intervention will have some signal or communication value. The computer manager felt that a transfer pricing mechanism that included costing of variations might have more signal value than a co-ordination committee.

The third point concerns initiative overload. Almost every company at one time or another has suffered from too many centrally driven initiatives. Business–unit managers either become overstretched working on multiple corporate projects and letting their own business priorities slip or they keep their heads down in the knowledge that the new initiative will soon be overtaken by the next 'flavour of the month'. Adding one more initiative can therefore sometimes have serious knock-on consequences for the overall climate in the company, even if it is sensible. If the organisation is already strung out with projects and other initiatives, the opportunity cost of one more may be much higher than a rational analysis would suggest. It may be the straw that breaks the organisation's back. This overload point has a clear link with the next category of knock-on effect, the impact on other parenting influences.

Other parenting influences

The most important dimension of parenting in most companies is the relationship between the chief executive or chief operating officer and the heads of the businesses. Often this relationship is a two or three-stage one. The CEO has division heads reporting into the centre, and business heads reporting to division heads.

These executive relationships have a big influence on the activities of the businesses. The influence of senior line managers affects many areas of decision making in the businesses: performance targets, strategies, appointments. We call these influences stand-alone parenting because they are the influence of the parent on businesses as stand-alone entities (see sidebar – 'What is stand-alone parenting?').

The knock-on issue is whether the proposed intervention will negatively or positively affect the stand-alone parenting relationship. Will the intervention make it easier or harder for the stand-alone parenting to be effective? Will it reinforce or undermine the current control process? Will it make it easier or harder to assess the major investment decisions? Will it help or hinder the centre in setting the right targets?

Understanding the impact an intervention may have on stand-alone parenting is not straightforward. It requires a knowledge of the people involved, the organisational context, and other details of the way the relationship works. However, there are two typical knock-on effects worth looking out for.

The first is a negative consequence. It often arises when the autonomy of a business unit is reduced. It is a particular danger in companies that add value from the corporate centre by creating a performance culture. They decentralise responsibility to well-defined business units and set stretching performance targets. They help their businesses achieve those targets, but reinforce the accountability of the business. Managers that don't clear the hurdle are squeezed out of the team, until the company has a cadre of managers who perform.

If synergy initiatives (e.g. tied supply relationships, transfer-pricing mechanisms, standard policies and co-ordinated strategies) reduce their autonomy, business unit managers may no longer feel totally account-

What is stand-alone parenting?

Stand-alone parenting consists of all the influences parent managers have on a business as a separate stand-alone unit. For example, it includes

- defining a unit's boundaries and mission
- approving and guiding a unit's strategy
- setting and agreeing budgets and performance targets
- monitoring performance against targets
- appointing the head of the unit and influencing other appointments within the unit
- approving, disapproving or seeking changes in capital expenditure requests
- setting policies and giving instructions to the unit as a stand-alone business
- reacting to performance issues and crises.

Stand-alone parenting is best understood in juxtaposition with synergy or linkage parenting. Synergy parenting involves influences by parent managers that only make sense if there are other businesses in the portfolio. Stand-alone parenting involves influences that would occur even if there were no other businesses in the portfolio.

Many activities of parent managers are a mix of both stand-alone parenting and linkage parenting. For example, an intervention to reduce manufacturing costs might involve some of the following:

- setting cost reduction targets for each business (stand-alone parenting)
- moving the manufacture of one product to a more suitable factory in another unit (linkage parenting)
- sharing progress on cost-reduction targets between businesses (linkage parenting)
- applying pressure on one unit to change its manufacturing manager (stand-alone parenting)
- centralising the purchasing of certain common raw materials (linkage parenting).

able. They may wonder why they should put their careers on the line for stretching targets when their ability to meet them is not totally in their control. They may therefore resist taking full responsibility for achieving targets. This makes it harder to create and sustain a performance culture, since managers have legitimate excuses for not delivering.

● In one company, the small and frugal centre decentralised to 100 or so business units, each targeted on a particular segment of the media industry. The company owned magazines, newspapers, radio stations and other media businesses. Each focused unit had complete autonomy over its business: what products to offer and how to market to its customers. The centre helped with central purchasing, but encouraged very few other internal links. The chief executive believed that the 'editorial team' should be the wealth-creating unit. Any linking activity that in his view clouded his view of the effectiveness of a team or threatened to cut across its responsibility was discouraged. As a result, the centre (including division levels for magazines, newspapers, radio and other businesses) consisted of no more than 60 people. And the company had performed ahead of its industry, and proved the value of its decentralised philosophy by improving the performance of acquisitions. Typically, the company cut overhead, decentralised to lower level managers and encouraged them to stretch for more growth and more profitability.

Company managers regularly put forward suggestions for improving links between businesses. One manager wanted to co-ordinate the marketing for all of the magazines into a central marketing function. Another wanted to centralise newspaper management, arguing that he could save overhead by treating each newspaper as a product within a larger business. A third wanted to rationalise magazine subscription departments, arguing that new technologies made it possible to add value to the company's large number of mailing lists. By and large, the CEO resisted these initiatives, fearing they would reduce accountability. He believed that creative people are apt to lose sight of commercial priorities unless they have full performance responsibility. Any clouding of accountability could cause them to pursue creative ends at the expense of profitability.

Although he didn't put it like this, the CEO was concerned about the impact on stand-alone parenting. Much of the value the parent was adding stemmed from its management philosophy, emphasising low overhead, high accountability and high performance. The pursuit of synergies (other than some central buying of supplies) could have a knock-on effect that far outweighed the benefits. Such concern for impacts on the stand-alone parenting relationship is common, particularly among companies where unit accountability is key to the parenting philosophy. This does not mean such firms should ignore all synergy possibilities. It does mean that interventions should be devised to get some of the benefit without weakening accountability.

The second typical knock-on effect is positive. Synergy initiatives can provide parent managers with a better understanding of the business units. Where the intervention requires the parent manager to spend more time and effort to get to grips with operating issues, increased awareness may well allow the parent manager to improve the quality of parenting.

● In one company, an internal benchmarking exercise confirmed that business units had similar overhead structures. But against external benchmarks parent managers found that the best practice in the industry was 25% better. By setting individual targets for each business unit they succeeded in lowering overhead to competitive levels. The benchmarking exercise, launched as a project to encourage sharing, yielded information that improved the company's stand-alone parenting.

These two typical knock-on effects – weakening accountability and improving parent managers' awareness – are examples of the consequences interventions can have for stand-alone parenting. They are often, but not always, present, depending on the specifics of the case.

In many situations, interventions involve a bundle of actions including both stand-alone (e.g. raise performance targets, change unit heads) and linkage parenting (e.g. form a co-ordination committee, appoint a central expert). The knock-on assessment is, then, about judging what impact this bundle of interventions will have on other parenting initiatives. The implications here are important. It is rare that parent managers can isolate a synergy initiative and consider it on its own, without reference to other parent initiatives. Interventions are normally hybrids, neither purely vertical nor purely horizontal in effect.

Motivation/innovation

The energy and creativity of an organisation are the product of delicately balanced inputs – shared ambitions, stimulating relationships, turned-on teams, leadership, beliefs and underlying values. Parental interventions can tip these delicate balances positively or negatively. The impact of control systems, policies, co-ordination loops and other tools of organisational bureaucracies is often to sap energy and dampen innovation. On the other hand, they can also promote teamwork and generate enthusiasm.

The knock-on issue is about whether the intervention will enhance or reduce motivation and innovation. Normally the two go together. An intervention that dismantles a fired-up team will demotivate the members and kill innovation (unless the members of the team find equally good working relationships elsewhere). An intervention that requires extra reporting and controls will sap energy (unless the controls add stretch ambitions and demand commitment). An intervention that constrains independent action in the name of co-ordination will discourage initiative (unless the participants form a team with shared ambitions and supportive norms). Most interventions have the potential both to reduce and enhance motivation and innovation – so parent managers need to design their interventions accordingly.

● In one company, a decision to link a group of European businesses in pursuit of economies in manufacturing, purchasing and marketing resulted in a clear loss of innovation. 'I was surprised about the degree to which the new organisation killed innovation in the first couple of years. This was partly a result of a decline in initiative as managers tried to understand their new roles,' commented one manager.

One of the projects was to create a Europe-wide technical organisation for process engineering and product development. Parent managers hoped the new organisation would eliminate duplication, reduce competition between local technical centres and increase critical mass in certain areas.

Instead of working within close-knit, geographically focused units, the group's technical specialists were now part of geographically spread project teams contributing to a Europe-wide agenda, led by remote managers. The result: loss of creativity and motivation. 'Technical people get their energy and enthusiasm from working closely with other technical people, feeding off their ideas and reinforcing enthusiasm. It's hard to create the same sort of team spirit when the members of the team are living in different countries and the boss of the team does not speak their language,' explained one technical project leader. Another commented: 'The new organisation has diminished some of the competitive energy that was a traditional part of European relationships. In the days when the UK factory and the French factory saw each other as rivals, an enormous amount of energy was put into advancing manufacturing practice.'

These quotes illustrate well the knock-on effects of this attempt to gain synergies. The intended benefits were indeed achieved, but the cost in terms of damage to motivation and innovation may have been greater, at least in the short term.

- In another example the parent manager deliberately chose an intervention that would minimise the effects of loss of motivation and innovation, even at the risk of losing some of the benefits. The opportunity concerned the use of the world-wide web for marketing purposes. A number of the company's media-oriented businesses were beginning to experiment with the web, and parent managers could see the potential for co-ordination. The chief executive realised that the cost of allowing all the companies to do their own experimenting would be high. Moreover, left to their own devices, some businesses would do it later than or worse than others.

  The chief executive's initial intention was to set up a central unit to chivvy the businesses, co-ordinate learning and form relationships with suppliers. However, he also had to bear in mind the toll in terms of dented motivation and innovation. Previous attempts to centralise activities had clearly weakened commitment in the businesses, which blamed the central unit when problems emerged. Motivation had plunged as the central unit and the businesses squabbled. In addition, he was concerned that the range of experimentation would be affected if the mindset of one central manager was imposed on the thinking of all the business units.

His solution was to create two centres of excellence, led by two of the larger business units. The other businesses were asked to align themselves with one or other of the centres with a view to sharing best practice, getting consistent advice and co-ordinating purchases. The two centres were also encouraged to co-ordinate where they saw mutual benefits.

As he expected, the two centres of excellence saw each other as healthy rivals, and the move generated strong commitment both within the units and with their group of aligned businesses. Despite the rivalry, however, they did co-ordinate over important issues such as the creation of a corporate web site, the purchasing of expensive computer-aided design equipment and the use of software. However, their thinking diverged in some areas, and the two units experimented with different marketing techniques.

At the time of writing, it is not clear whether the additional experimentation has paid off in money terms, but it is clear that the decentralised, multi-node intervention succeeded in gaining some co-ordination while at the same time generating energy and commitment maintaining innovation.

Most interventions affect motivation and innovation to some degree. Often, the effect is minor and unimportant. Sometimes, it is major and should be taken into account in designing the intervention. A major knock-on effect is likely when motivation or innovation is an important ingredient in business performance and when the intervention affects one of the driving influences of these factors.

The driving influences behind motivation and innovation depend on the circumstances of the organisation and the individuals who work in it. Sometimes internal competition may be the key influence. Or it may be a shared vision. Often motivation and innovation depend on the close working relationships of a group of individuals. Sometimes they depend on local identity, where the enemy is the larger bureaucracy. Sometimes, the enemy is an identifiable competitor.

To determine whether an intervention will have a big impact on commitment or creativity, parent managers need to understand both the role that these factors play in achieving high performance, and the way the organisation and individuals work. While this level of detailed knowledge is hard to get at, it is clear that the possible impact on motivation and innovation cannot be left out of the equation.

Summary

This chapter describes our fourth and last mental discipline – assessing how far the benefits of a planned synergy might be dissipated by knock-on effects. We emphasise this discipline because we have noted that parent managers often fail to take account of the possible downside to their interventions, which can be large and emerge in unexpected places. Knock-on effects can be positive as well. But while we recommend a balanced assessment, the synergy biases make it particularly important to dwell on the often-overlooked downsides.

We define four categories of knock-on effect – the impacts on business mindsets, organisational dynamics, other parenting influences, and motivation and innovation. There are no foolproof ways of identifying knock-on effects or finding interventions that amplify positive effects and damp down negative ones. We are not therefore offering short cuts or analytical tools for making the judgements. Our concern is with the systematic lack of attention to negative effects and the need for parent managers to strike a balance. Biased thinking can be the result of either an over-optimistic starting position or a lack of understanding of the likely knock-on effects. The aim of our discipline is to correct the bias by suggesting a framework of four categories for managers to think about.

6
Deciding What to Do

In situations where an intuitive decision is not sufficient, managers can use a more structured process for choosing interventions.

First, managers need to 'size the prize' and 'pinpoint the parenting opportunity'. When the prize is small or there is no parenting opportunity, no intervention is necessary. When the prize or the parenting opportunity is uncertain, an 'exploratory' intervention is called for.

If the prize is substantial and the parenting opportunity clear, managers then need to define three alternative interventions that address the parenting opportunity.

The final step is to evaluate these three interventions against three criteria – impact on the parenting opportunity, ease of implementation and knock-on effects. If all interventions have high implementation or downside risks, no action should be taken. Otherwise a choice is made by considering which intervention will give the best overall outcome.

The main purpose of this book is to help managers choose better interventions; to help them make better decisions about how they manage synergies. We hope that in some cases our observations will dissuade managers from making any interventions at all. This could be because the prize is too small, there is no parenting opportunity, the parent does not have the skills necessary to make an effective intervention, or the knock-on effects are likely to outweigh the benefits. In most cases, however, we anticipate that the effect of thinking more deeply will be to produce an intervention that yields a better net outcome for the organisation as a whole.

In our opening chapter, we explained why synergies are so elusive and frustrating: why parent company managers find it hard to create the cross-company collaborations they would like to see happen. The next four chapters describe four mental disciplines that parent managers can use to help them in making a decision. We are not suggesting in these chapters a rigorous analytical process. Rather we are offering four ways of thinking. Most managers make decisions in a holistic, intuitive way. They expose themselves to the issue and then, drawing on their knowledge of the people, the organisation and the company's strategy, they intuitively synthesize some intervention. Managers do not have time (or interest) for rigorous analysis or exhaustive review of all the options. Yet there are circumstances where some structured analysis and at least some formal comparison of options can be valuable.

This chapter therefore describes a practical tool which allows managers to be more structured and analytical (Exhibit 6.1). The tool is a decision aid that harnesses the four mental disciplines into a flow chart with three possible outcomes – choose an 'implementation' intervention; choose an 'exploratory' intervention; do nothing.

The flow chart starts with the mental discipline of 'sizing the prize'. Parent managers faced with the urge to intervene need to articulate the primary benefit and estimate its value. If the benefit is small, the answer is probably to do nothing. If the benefit is unclear, the answer is to do something that will elucidate more information about the benefit – an

Exhibit 6.1   Choosing interventions.

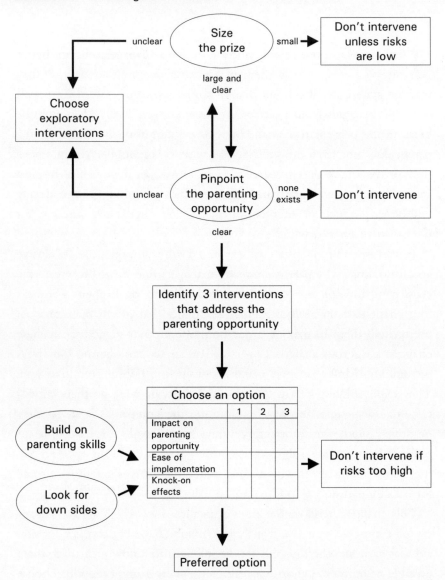

exploratory mechanism. If the benefit is large, the next step is to pinpoint the parenting opportunity.

At this point in the flow chart there are again three possible outcomes. If there is no parenting opportunity, the answer is leave well alone. If the parenting opportunity is unclear, explore the issues further. If the parenting opportunity is clear, move on to identify the intervention options.

With clarity about the benefit and the parenting opportunity, managers can narrow down the choice of intervention. But there will still be options. So the next step is to identify some reasonable options. We suggest that three possible options should be selected, and compared with each other in a simple evaluation grid. The grid has three evaluation criteria – the degree to which the option addresses the parenting opportunity (and hence releases the benefit), the ease with which the option can be implemented, and the balance of knock-on effects.

Even at this point parent managers may still decide not to intervene. The difficulties of implementation and the risks of downsides may outweigh the potential benefits. Normally, however, a preferred option emerges from the evaluation grid.

In practice, we would expect managers to use the flow chart mainly for major decisions where they are uncertain what to do or to review conflicting ideas put forward by other managers. Not all decisions need to be 'put through' the flow chart. Yet we know from experience that managers have found this chart useful in enabling them to think through the pros and cons of alternative interventions. It also provides a structure for communicating the rationale for judgements that have been made.

The circles in the flow chart (the four mental disciplines) have been fully described in Chapters 2–5. In consequence, this chapter will focus on the rectangular boxes, structured around the three possible outcomes – no intervention, an 'exploratory' intervention, and the choice of a preferred 'implementation' intervention.

When not to intervene

Perhaps paradoxically, one of the major contributions of this book, we believe, is the advice to do nothing when intervening is not clearly beneficial. There are three situations when it is better not to intervene. First, and most important, is when there is no identifiable parenting opportunity. Second is when the likely benefit is small. Third is when the interventions that address the parenting opportunity involve too much risk: implementation has a low chance of success or knock-on effects could be very harmful.

No parenting opportunity

In Chapter 3, we showed how managers can identify parenting opportunities. We pointed out that the only logic for an intervention is the existence of a parenting opportunity – an opportunity for the parent company to do something which the individual businesses for some reason cannot do on their own. In the absence of a parenting opportunity, the natural, self-interested, profit-seeking behaviours of business unit managers will cause them to create whatever synergies are appropriate. It is the existence of a parenting opportunity that justifies intervening. When there is no parenting opportunity, interventions are likely to destroy value rather than create it.

The sidebar – 'No parenting opportunity – describes a parent manager whose enthusiasm for synergy (synergy bias) and belief in the need to take action (parenting presumption) causes him to intervene even though there is no parenting opportunity. The net result is negative. The interventions end up making it harder for the business units to work together, because they interfere with the self-interested relationships that would normally have operated.

Small benefits

In Chapter 2, we argued that parent managers needed to define clear benefits and look for those where the payoff is substantial. The implication is that small benefits should be ignored. Given a choice, why not focus on synergies with big benefits? In a broad sense, this is good advice. Parent managers are too busy (or should be too busy) to mess around with situations where the benefits are small. The general rule, then, is to ignore small benefits. But, as with all general rules, there are circumstances where this one is wrong.

The reason for avoiding small benefits is risk. Because opportunity costs, knock-on effects and implementation problems are hard to predict, there is a risk that small benefits will be eaten up. In some situations, however, opportunity costs are trivial, implementation predictable, and

Sidebar 6.1   No parenting opportunity

The chief executive of a group of professional service businesses wanted to encourage more cross-fertilisation and joint working between his five subsidiaries. His ambition was based on an insight he had had earlier in his career. He had worked on two major cross-unit initiatives. One had involved work for the Russian government, another had involved setting up a management-training business drawing on the expertise in the other four businesses. He had found these two experiences very exciting. He personally had learned a great deal from working with a cross-unit project team and he had sensed the togetherness and purpose that these projects had created. He felt that there was a great deal of synergy to be released if consultants from the five businesses would work together more often.

In order to encourage cross-working, he had tried a number of interventions. First, he established a standard transfer-pricing system between the businesses at a rate low enough to encourage businesses to use professionals from other businesses. Second, he had gradually equalised the human resource policies of the different businesses to make transfers between businesses easier. Third, he personally promoted and encouraged projects that brought professionals together from the different businesses. The net results of his efforts were, however, probably negative. Cross-unit working would probably have been greater if the chief executive had not intervened at all!

The transfer-pricing system encouraged business units to ask for help from other units; but it discouraged units from giving it. Since the transfer price was attractive to the unit buying help, it was automatically unattractive to the seller. Since the culture frowned on individuals refusing assistance, the transfer-pricing system was causing dysfunctional behaviour. The most valuable individuals, whose time billed out to clients at the highest rate, were actively avoiding developing relationships with other units so that they wouldn't be asked for help. The opportunity cost of doing internal work was too high.

At the same time, unit managers were beginning to stop asking for help, for two reasons. Some stopped because, having been rejected in the past, they did not want to approach 'those stuck up prima donnas again'. Others recognised that asking for help was the equivalent of asking for a favour. They reduced their requests so as not to impose on managers in other units.

The equalisation of human-resource policies also had a negative effect. It indeed made it easier to move people between units, but it was causing trouble for businesses like top management counselling that habitually charged higher rates and recruited more senior consultants. These businesses were finding it hard to recruit on the standard conditions and had had to introduce a complex bonus and payment scheme to 'get around' them.

Moreover, the standard policies had another harmful effect. They communicated to the professionals in all the businesses that they were equal, that they should be ambitious to be able to move across units, and that they ought to be able to do each others' work. Since the top management counselling business had higher status, many professionals applied to join and were dissatisfied at being rejected. This both damaged morale and caused the counselling business to distance itself from the unwanted attentions of other businesses.

The chief executive's third intervention was to go out of his way to foster cross-unit projects. This had the perverse effect of reducing their number and even causing some projects to go 'underground'. Some managers saw the attention from the chief executive as unhelpful. His involvement meant that everything took more time. Then, the chief executive would usually try to expand the project to include more units or a broader scope, often blurring the original objective. As a result, some professionals avoided cross-unit projects and others were doing them as skunk works, out of the limelight.

The story was not all negative. Some cross-unit projects blossomed under the chief executive's attentions, and his enthusiasm for cross-unit working was infectious to some professionals. However, the disadvantages appeared to outweigh the advantages. The chief executive's mistake was not his enthusiasm for joint working. His mistake was to ignore the parenting opportunity rule. If there is no clear parenting opportunity, resist the temptation. Do not intervene.

In this case, there were no blockages to remove and no other obvious opportunity to use parental skills. The professionals regularly worked with each other across units when it made sense. In fact, cross-unit working was normal as groups of professionals assembled the appropriate resources for each assignment. There was no reason to suppose that the units were doing too little cross-unit work. The number of cross-unit projects had declined since the time when the chief executive himself was in a business unit but there were sound commercial reasons for that. The units were now larger and more self sufficient. And there were fewer new-territory and new-business projects because the firm was more mature.

Without a parenting opportunity, the chief executive would have done better to have left well alone. His enthusiasm for joint working would have been sufficient example, and might well have had a net beneficial effect if he had limited his efforts to celebrating joint initiatives, rather than intervening.

negative knock-on effects insignificant: the risk is low. Four conditions therefore need to exist for a small benefit to warrant an intervention:

- the benefit must be certain;
- opportunity costs must be non-existent or predictable;
- implementation problems must be negligible;
- negative knock-on effects must be unlikely.

Examples of small benefits with low risk often exist in administrative functions. Centralising management of the pension fund does not create large savings and is not strategically important. However, it may make sense to intervene in a unit which still manages its own pensions when the benefit of centralising is clear and measurable: no scarce resources (i.e. opportunity costs) are involved; there are no implementation issues (e.g. there is already a central pension provided to other units); and there is no danger of the transfer of responsibility backfiring in other areas.

Tax, foreign exchange, cash-flow management and payroll administration fall into this category of small benefits with low risk. However, many other central administrative activities are potentially high risk. For example, centralising activities such as public relations, human resource policies and strategic–planning formats entails high risk because it may involve:

• substantial senior management time in discussing and settling the issues;
• potential implementation problems if some businesses resist the co-ordinated approach;
• significant knock–on effects as a result of contamination and loss of motivation.

Centralisation in high–risk areas should only be carried out if the benefits are clear and large.

Small, low-risk synergies are not only found in administrative activities. They can occur in any type of link-up.

● For example, a company with a number of magazine businesses proposed that they join forces to market their databases.

Each magazine had a subscription list, giving it a valuable up-to-date list of names. Most units did not put much effort in to selling these lists since they only brought in small revenues. In the main, they gave their lists to list brokers. Selling mailing lists was not a strategic priority for any of the businesses.

The chief executive believed that there would be a small but clear benefit from co-ordinating the marketing of these databases: sales of lists would increase, commissions to list brokers would be reduced, and expertise might be gained in exploiting the resource. The problem was to find a way of intervening that had low risk.

The solution was simple: to create an internal list broker. From the business-unit point of view the mechanism was exactly the same as before, so managers did not need to spend more time on it. Likewise the parent manager's time spent on the initiative was kept to a minimum by hiring a full-time specialist to do the job. Knock-on effects were largely absent and implementation problems easy to solve: if the internal unit gave bad service, the businesses could revert to their previous arrangements.

Interventions to pursue small benefit linkages can therefore be desirable. However, they should be put on the agenda only after they have met the qualifying conditions. Too often, parent managers devote too much time to 'tidying up' small areas of synergy benefit, ignoring the opportunity cost of their time and the risks involved, with the result that the net outcome is negative.

High risk situations

The third situation in which no action is the best decision is where the only interventions that will address the parenting opportunity are too risky. The risk can take two forms: implementation problems and excessive knock-on risks.

Implementation problems arise because parent managers do not have the skills or knowledge needed to make the intervention work.

● For example, an electrical engineering group had recently seen a change in its marketplace. In a traditionally regulated sector, the group's businesses had virtual monopolies in their respective market segments. With deregulation, the businesses were now competing for work.

One of the biggest opportunities for improvement was purchasing: components and equipment often amounted to 60% or more of the contract. A consultant's report suggested that purchasing improvements could take out millions of dollars of cost. Because none of the businesses had high purchasing skills, the parent organisation perceived an opportunity to co-ordinate the function, raising skill levels across the businesses and gaining economies of scale.

Unfortunately, however, parent managers had no more skill in purchasing than the business managers. What's more, politics rather than an assessment of competence meant that responsibility for developing the central purchasing function would be likely to be given to the wrong person. The consultant, therefore, recommended that the parent company should not intervene at all. The units should be left to develop their own purchasing skills as best they could. The consultant judged that the

parent's skill levels were so low in this area that intervention could well
do more harm than good.

Few parent managers are confident enough to acknowledge their own
skill weaknesses. But objectivity is necessary to avoid interventions that
fall over at the implementation stage. The mental discipline of reviewing
parenting skills helps. It encourages parent managers to look for interventions that match their skill levels. It makes parent managers wary of
pushing ahead with interventions unless they are 'well-grooved' or supported by 'natural champions'. If neither of these two implementation
conditions is present, we urge parent managers seriously to consider the
option of doing nothing. Pushing ahead with an intervention in the face
of skill deficiencies is often more dangerous than letting the status quo
continue.

Excessive knock-on risks are common when the intervention entails changing managers. For example, in situations where the chemistry between
managers is preventing an opportunity from being exploited, the only
realistic solution may be to move one or both to other jobs. However,
these managers may be perfectly competent in other dimensions of their
jobs, and moving them thus can have large possible downsides.

The risk of substantial indirect effects also occurs when a large core
unit links up with a small, new and different unit. The two businesses
may have opportunities to co-ordinate purchasing, share distribution or
sell to common customers. The problem occurs because the larger, more
established unit dominates the linkage, making insufficient allowance
for differences between the units or contaminating the thinking of the
smaller unit.

In both cases, it may be better not to intervene at all. The risk of
excessive knock-on effects is too high. It may seem defeatist to sub-
optimise deliberately, but it may be the wisest decision. The danger is to
look for ways round the knock-on risk, without fully addressing it. For
example, to get around personal incompatibilities between business unit
heads, parent managers sometimes try to involve more junior managers.
These managers are often enthusiastic about co-ordinating with their
peers, but the solution rarely works. Normally, implementation at some

point needs support from the business unit heads and it is not forthcoming. All that happens is that the initiative absorbs a good deal of management time and emotional energy to no purpose. Moreover, junior managers are apt to be demotivated by the experience.

To counteract the influence of large dominant units, parent managers sometimes intervene directly themselves. In practice, this is also problematic. The parent manager's thinking is normally influenced by the policies and behaviours of the dominant unit. Attempts by the parent manager to intervene on behalf of the smaller units therefore often compound the error rather than correct it.

There are many other causes of negative knock-on effects, as discussed in Chapter 5. When the risks are high and difficult to avoid, it is better to eschew intervention and devote parenting energy to more promising opportunities.

When to choose exploratory interventions

When the prize or the parenting opportunity is uncertain, we recommend a cautious or exploratory approach. As we pointed out in Chapters 2 and 3, defining the prize and understanding the parenting opportunity are not easy tasks. Frequently the conclusion is unclear. Will a combined sales force produce net benefits or net costs? Is the German product manager resisting the standard marketing campaign because of NIH or because Germany is different? Is the lack of interest in new media opportunities the result of blinkered focus on existing products, large opportunity costs, lack of incentives to take risk, or a sober judgement that the opportunities are small or the business skills inappropriate?

Frequently parent managers can give only approximate replies to these questions. Yet the interventions depend on their answers. How to proceed in such cases? They should take actions that reduce the uncertainty: see if the benefits are really there, find out more about opportunity costs and learn more about the parenting opportunity. They should make an exploratory intervention.

An exploratory intervention is an action designed to give the parent manager more information. It may be set up to test whether a benefit is real or substantial, to gain more insight into the reasons why the businesses are not spontaneously working together, or to try out a given intervention. Exploratory interventions should be designed to accumulate information, test hypotheses, and generate early feedback.

Exploratory interventions differ from implementation interventions more in intention than in choice of mechanism. Exhibit 6.2 is a sample list of explanatory interventions. Some of them could be used in either implementation or exploratory mode, depending on the parent manager's intention. Being clear about intention is therefore important. For example, one parent manager might suggest fact-finding visits between two factories as a way of learning more about the size of benefits from best-practice sharing (i.e. as an exploratory mechanism). Another parent manager, who knew that benefits from best-practice sharing were large, might see a programme of visits as the best way to encourage sharing (i.e. an implementation mechanism).

Exhibit 6.2   Example exploratory interventions.

- Pilot projects
- Fact-finding visits
- Exploratory committees
- Temporary appointments
- Time-limited mechanisms
- Experimental initiatives
- Gatherings and forums
- Communication committees
- Informal suggestions
- Piggyback other mechanisms
  - i   training programmes
  - ii   management meetings
  - iii   committees
  - iv   central functions

Depending on the parent manager's intention therefore fact-finding visits can be either an implementation intervention or an exploratory intervention. In practice interventions are often a bit of both. The value of distinguishing between the two objectives is the additional clarity of purpose gained. The key feature of exploratory mechanisms is that information about benefits, parenting opportunities, skills or knock-on effects is part of their purpose. The end result of a good exploratory intervention is a better informed parent manager.

We have five pieces of practical advice on exploratory interventions.

1   *Confirm the parenting opportunity first.* If the parenting opportunity is unclear, the first exploratory task is to understand it better. Try informing the business units of the proposed initiative to see if it is a 'perception opportunity'. Unpick their cost/benefit calculations to see if it is an 'evaluation opportunity'. Learn more about motivations and implementation skills to take a view on whether it is a 'motivation or implementation opportunity'. Only intervene further when there is a clear hypothesis about the parenting opportunity.

The natural instinct of parent managers faced with uncertainty is to attempt to clarify the benefit. 'I need to understand the benefit better. Once the benefit is clear we should have no problem persuading the businesses to fall in line.' But it is not necessary for the parent manager to have 20/20 vision about the benefit. It helps, as we have been at pains to point out in Chapter 2. But if the benefit is inherently uncertain, the business managers are normally in the best position to judge whether it is worthwhile or not. The parent manager's job in these circumstances is to ensure that nothing is impeding business managers, and then let them get on with it. In uncertain situations it is therefore best to focus first on understanding more about the parenting opportunity.

2   *Use or create well-grooved mechanisms.* In Chapter 5, we explained the importance of well-grooved mechanisms: they reduce the risk that interventions will flounder because of implementation problems. The same principles are relevant for exploratory interventions: well-grooved exploratory interventions are more likely to work than

new ones. Parent managers know how to get the information they need from the mechanisms, and business unit managers know what is expected of them.

At Canon, there is a hierarchy of different types of project teams for first exploring and then implementing cross-business product developments (see Chapter 4, page 108). 'Working Groups' are used mainly for exploring new-product potential, while 'Major Project Teams' are used mainly for implementation. In other companies, the exploratory and implementation interventions may not be so well separated, yet parent managers and business managers can still be clear about the two different objectives. Unilever has a tradition of using cross-unit working groups, chaired by a parent manager, as both exploratory and implementation interventions. When the 'Personal Products Coordination' decided to explore the potential for synergy between the sales forces in Europe, the first initiative was to form a working group. This group not only explored the potential for joint training and co-ordinating prices, it also went on to implement some initiatives. In this situation it is important that the managers involved are skilled at switching between exploratory mode and implementation mode.

In companies with less experience, the differences between exploratory and implementation interventions may need to be carefully signalled. Business managers need to know what is intended and what influence they will have on the process. Because of the problems of parenting bias and parenting presumption, business managers are frequently wary of cross-company initiatives. 'If we don't knock this on the head quickly, we will be spending all our time in co-ordination meetings,' explained one business-unit manager who had been invited to attend a marketing co-ordination forum. Business managers often see interventions as the thin end of a wedge, which will lead to loss of freedom and flexibility and greater control. This can cause them to derail exploratory interventions if they do not understand their learning objective.

The benefit of well-grooved mechanisms is that they signal clearly what the parent manager's intentions are, what the process of exploration is likely to be, and what control the business managers will have over the conclusions. Without a well-grooved mechanism, parent managers need other ways of making these elements of the process clear.

3   *Piggyback other mechanisms.* Exploratory interventions can be expensive. Hiring a consultant to benchmark manufacturing performance across five sites will cost megabucks. Putting together a working group to examine the potential for common purchasing can also be expensive. Even organising a management conference or functional forum is costly. When the opportunity cost of management time is similar to the billing rate of a quality consultant, exploration costs should be a major factor in the decision about what to do.

Piggybacking is one way of keeping costs down. An existing co-ordination group can be used to explore new areas of co-ordination. Management development exercises can be used to explore synergy potential. Exploratory items can go on the agendas of management conferences. There are many ways of piggybacking existing mechanisms. This is why for many companies, such as Unilever, exploratory and implementation mechanisms overlap.

The danger of piggybacking is the confusion it can cause in the minds of business managers (or parent managers responsible for the mechanism). Unless the mechanism is regularly used for dual purposes, it is important to signal what is planned and why.

4   *Ensure sufficient resources.* While piggybacking is an excellent way of keeping the cost of exploration down, it also has dangers. Piggybacking can mean that exploration is starved of adequate resources. Some opportunities need thorough examination before any action is taken. Best-practice sharing is an example. Understanding the size of the benefit from standardising practices across five factories can take a small project team of managers or consultants a number of man-months or even more. The danger is that the task is given to an assistant factory manager who has many other responsibilities and no staff. In other words, the detailed analysis never gets done.

This is a problem we have encountered many times. Parent managers have spotted areas of likely benefit and have initiated exploratory action, but without devoting adequate resources to the issue. As a result there is endless and inconclusive debate between the parent manager and the business managers about the nature of the opportunity, the size of the benefit, and what, if anything, should be done about it.

If exploration is warranted, do it with the determination and resources necessary to obtain the information that is required.

5 *Use time-limited mechanisms.* Something that starts out as an exploration can all too easily end up as a time-wasting talking shop. In many companies managers told us about communication committees, liaison groups and functional forums that were set up to explore synergies, but turned into major time-wasters. The first few meetings were stimulating, generating new ideas and relationships, but since no process for ending proceedings had been defined at the start, they continued long after the rationale had disappeared.

Another frequent problem arises from central appointments. Corporate appoints a parent manager to explore synergy opportunities in marketing, engineering or new-product development. In the first few months, the parent manager makes a major contribution, identifying areas that had been overlooked, creating relationships where none had existed before, and stimulating a search for better practice. But after this initial spurt of value added, the job sinks into an administrative routine which adds little but uses up a great deal of time.

The solution to these problems is time-limited interventions. Any intervention that is primarily exploratory should have a stated time limit and a process for bringing it to an end. Committees, project teams, work groups, central appointments and information systems should have stop as well as start dates if they are set up to explore rather than implement a link.

The second benefit of a time-limited mechanism is the signal it sends to business-level managers: this intervention is exploratory. The extra time commitment, loss of autonomy, and additional responsibility is in the first instance only temporary. Whether they become permanent depends on a decision within a determined time frame. This is reassuring to hard-pressed managers for whom such activities are an addition to an already heavy burden.

The third benefit of time-limited mechanisms is that they oblige parent managers to come to grips with hard decisions. Who decides what to do next? What information is essential to make the decision? Exploratory interventions have a purpose: to help parent managers decide what to do about a particular synergy issue. Without a time limit, it is easy for managers to lose sight of this. Like all deadlines, a time limit concentrates the mind.

In implementation interventions, the parent manager has clearly defined what he or she wants to happen – standardise the brand logo, reduce administration costs, increase cross-selling of products – and identified an initiative to carry it out. In an exploratory intervention, the parent manager's thinking is different. Unsure what she is trying to achieve, she is in discovery mode. A side-effect of the intervention may help participants learn more about the issue, but the prime object of an exploratory intervention is to help the parent manager obtain more information about benefits, the nature of the parenting opportunity, and other factors that will help her decide what to do. Exploratory interventions are about making uncertainties manageable.

Identify options

In our decision flow chart (Exhibit 6.1), we suggest that decision-makers define three different possible ways of intervening. Each separate strategy for addressing the parenting opportunity and releasing the benefits will be likely to comprise a number of related interventions: a bundle of actions aimed to achieve the objective. For example, if the aim is to improve inter-trading between units, the three options might be to:

- define a transfer pricing policy, set up a liaison group to discuss the policy, identify exceptions, apply pressure to manager A who is not co-operating, and design a process for changing the policy in the future;

- review costing information to ensure compatibility, encourage open-book negotiations between the units, apply pressure to manager A who is not co-operating, and be available to listen to appeals against unfair negotiating tactics;
- insist on arms-length negotiations, allow businesses to source from outside the company, insist that internal suppliers are given the opportunity to compete fairly, apply pressure to manager A who is not co-operating.

We encourage managers to identify three intervention options because like any brainstorming activity identifying alternatives aids creativity. Not only does it reduce the danger of a blinkered single focus, but when the options are evaluated, further creativity often results from combining the best ideas from each. On the other hand, attempts to define more than three options can make the evaluation process too cumbersome. Three options is a practical number to evaluate.

For any given role, there are usually several possible interventions. Parent managers could counter lack of information about sales activities across units by one or a combination of the following interventions:

- ensure that all businesses produce literature on their activities and circulate it to each other;
- require companies to circulate sales visit reports and sales figures for all overlapping customers;
- sponsor a conference for senior sales people to address opportunities for collaboration;
- set up a central marketing function to orchestrate co-operation around strategic customers;
- create a shared sales force for key accounts.

This list of possible interventions is not intended to be exhaustive, nor does it bring out all of the ways in which each option could be implemented. It shows that the role to be played by the parent does not predetermine the specific intervention that the parent should make.

In fact, identifying the parenting opportunity can be as useful in opening up creative thinking about intervention options as in narrowing down the choice between options. Once the role for the parent is defined, it is then worthwhile not only to rule out unsuitable interventions, but also to brainstorm a list of different initiatives that could fulfil the role. In this way, managers can push options onto the table that they might otherwise have overlooked.

The choice of options will also depend on the nature of the benefit being addressed. If the benefit is about international brand development, it makes no sense to standardise financial-accounting procedures. If the benefit is about co-ordinating mail shots, combining sales forces is irrelevant. But, as with the parenting opportunity, a clear definition of the benefit does not lead to a single intervention option. To develop international brands, the intervention options could range from centralising brand management to encouraging more networking between brand managers. To co-ordinate mail shots, the options could range from setting up a combined direct-mail unit to encouraging the marketing managers of different units to talk to each other.

In other words, even if the first two mental disciplines have been properly applied, there will still be a range of options to chose from. Even if the benefit is clearly defined and the parenting opportunity well understood, choices need to be made.

How does a parent manager decide which three options to consider? The answer is often straightforward: three options are obvious possibilities. When this is not the case, the parent manager may either be faced with a confusingly wide range of possible options that need to be evaluated, or fixed in a blinkered way on a single option.

In an electricity distribution company, there was a problem between the business unit which managed the main assets, the wires and pylons of the distribution network, and the business unit that carried out the engineering works. The businesses had been separated because of the diversity of the skills and tasks, and because an increasing percentage of the engineering work was being outsourced. The division manager in charge of these units recognised that there was an opportunity to improve purchasing of supplies. Historically the company had never given much attention to this issue and, with the rise of a few global suppliers such as ABB, had begun to experience some sharp increases in equipment costs. The division manager wanted to bring in new purchasing skills, raise the profile of the purchasing managers, and improve co-ordination between the units.

This solution was to give responsibility for purchasing to either the network unit or the engineering unit.

In fact, there were many other options: he could have centralised purchasing at division level; changed the performance-measurement system to reduce rivalry between the units and encouraged them to share more information; upgraded the purchasing function in both units; or created a company-wide purchasing professional group.

Exhibit 6.3 Linkage interventions.

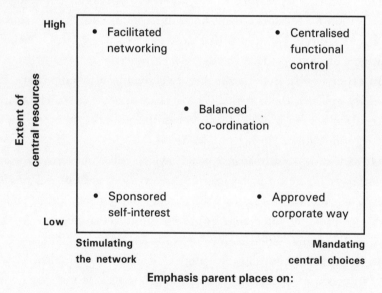

The value of defining three options is that it can assist parent managers out of this kind of dilemma. For example, a third option could be developed by:

- reconsidering the parenting opportunity or primary benefit (e.g. what ways are there to co-ordinate purchasing?);
- considering an option that involves much more centralisation (e.g. create a centralised purchasing function);
- considering an option that involves much less centralisation (e.g. encourage more networking).

Exhibit 6.3 is a useful tool for helping to generate additional options and for reducing a confusing range of choices to a few generics. It identifies two dimensions – the degree of central mandate and the extent of central staffs – and describes five generic interventions: sponsored self-interest, balanced co-ordination, centralised functional control, approved corporate way, and facilitated networking. The division manager of the electricity company could have used this matrix to define the following generic interventions.

- Set up a central purchasing function either at the centre or in one of the two businesses (centralised functional control).
- Encourage the businesses to hire new purchasing people and set up central policies to ensure co-ordination and promote professionalism (balanced co-ordination).
- Hire a central purchasing manager to act as guide and facilitator to managers in the businesses (facilitated networking).
- Define the improvements he felt each business should be able to achieve by upgrading its purchasing and improving co-ordination. Then set targets and policies for the businesses to follow (approved corporate way).
- Help develop relationships between the two businesses and with an outside consultant, in the hope that they would discover the need to upgrade and co-ordinate (sponsored self-interest).

The division manager would quickly have been able to eliminate the third option because it would create two layers of purchasing managers, something the division manager was strongly opposed to. He would also have eliminated the last option as being unlikely to have much impact. This would have left him with three broad options to evaluate in more detail.

Choose an option

The final part of the decision flow chart is to choose an option. We use a simple evaluation matrix.

Along the top of the matrix are columns for the three intervention options. Down the side of the matrix are three criteria against which the options need to be scored: the degree to which the option addresses the parenting opportunity; the ease with which the option can be implemented; and the net impact of likely knock-on effects. Each intervention (or bundle of interventions) should be scored against each of these criteria.

Two ways of scoring can help decision making. The first involves comparing the options against each other on all three criteria. The second involves choosing an option based on the first two criteria and then assessing the likely benefits against knock-on risks.

In the first method each option is scored relative to the other options. Score each option 'best', 'middle' or 'worst' for each criterion. Where two options score the same, the result will be two 'bests' and a 'middle' or a 'best' and two 'middles'. If one option scores 'best' on all three criteria, it is the preferred choice. If, however, the scores are mixed, you must make a judgement based on some weighting of the different scores. We have found it useful to search hard for an option that scores 'best' on all of the criteria. This reduces the need to make a judgement about the appropriate weighting. It also encourages creativity.

The second method is particularly useful in cases where the scores are mixed and where there is some possibility that the risks may outweigh the benefits. Here the options are scored on the first two criteria only. A preferred option is chosen based on the value of the benefit that is likely to result. If the option perfectly addresses the parenting opportunity and is easy to implement, 100% of the benefit will result. If the option addresses the parenting opportunity imperfectly and is likely to be difficult to implement, only 50% or less of the benefit may be achievable.

With a preferred option and an estimate of the likely benefit in financial terms (e.g. £100,000 extra profit a year or £5 million impact on shareholder value), managers can make a judgement about knock-on effects. What are the likely knock-on effects? Will they be high enough to negate the benefits? If the probability is high, the decision should be to do nothing, unless a better option can be found. If the probability is low, the preferred option is the right choice.

Both these methods are aids to decision making. They do not replace the need for balanced judgements taking into account all the factors involved. They can be used to aid the balanced judgements, and they are particularly helpful in situations where managers need to communicate their judgements or expose their thinking to challenge by managers with different views.

Use the evaluation matrix, too, to spur creativity. The search for an option that scores best on all three criteria is one device for forcing creativity. Another is to take each criterion in turn and think of options that will maximise the positives and minimise the negatives. In the sidebar – 'New technologies in retailing' – the CEO also used a third approach to spur creativity. He tried sequencing some of his intervention ideas to get the maximum impact with the minimum downside.

To promote co-ordination on database marketing and internet retailing, he first set up a co-ordination committee with two enthusiastic and skilled businesses. Then he sponsored a consultant-led project to understand the potential, persuading two more businesses to support the project. Then he applied pressure in the planning process to launch two co-ordinated 'learning' projects. Finally, in the long term he is expecting to centralise some activities in order to get substantially ahead of competitors, but he does not feel that the timing for this is yet right.

New technologies in retailing

The CEO of a diversified retailing company was trying to decide what to do about new technologies such as database marketing and on-line shopping. He was worried that each of his 5 businesses were giving these new technologies too little attention. He felt sure that there was an opportunity to use the size and diversity of the group not only to invest more in this new area but also to co-ordinate learning and generate economies of scale.

While there was great uncertainty about the exact size of the prize, the CEO was convinced that there would be large commercial benefits if he could gain an advantage in these new technologies.

The opportunity was framed as being 'how to co-ordinate the efforts of the businesses so as to gain an advantage in exploiting new technologies'. Debate initially focused on whether these technologies provided a significant commercial opportunity and whether co-ordination across the businesses would help to gain an advantage. At this level of aggregation it was easy for managers to disagree. Disaggregation helped with the debate and the CEO decided to focus on two specific areas of opportunity 'collection of information about customers to aid the selling of products through both existing retail formats and direct' and 'internet retailing'.

Exhibit 6.4   Defining parenting opportunities.

Categories of parenting opportunity	Specific causes
Perception opportunity	Lack of understanding
Evaluation opportunity	Short-term bias Anti-collaboration bias
Motivation opportunity	Short-term bias
Implementation opportunity	No internal champion in three out of five businesses

While the CEO recognised that the size of the prize in these two areas was uncertain and that his interventions needed to help understand the potential, he was convinced that the prize from co-ordination would be large and therefore he was looking for a way of implementing something rather than just exploring the potential.

The first problem was to clarify the parenting opportunity. Why was any intervention necessary? The CEO felt that there were parenting opportunities in all categories (Exhibit 6.4).

Because the managers of the businesses understood little about the opportunities, there was a lack of understanding of the possible benefits from co-ordination. There were also two reasons why the businesses might be mis-evaluating the opportunity: their focus on annual profits might cause them to place too high a discount factor on longer term revenues; their distaste for co-ordination, from a previous bad experience, might be causing them to allocate too high a cost to co-ordination efforts. The incentive scheme based on annual bonuses might also be causing managers who had evaluated the potential correctly to decide to delay action (and resist co-ordination) so as not to reduce their personal bonus. Finally, three of the businesses had no-one on their staff who was capable of championing database marketing or internet retailing. Hence these businesses did not have the skills needed to co-ordinate with their sister companies.

The next step was to think of some interventions that would address the parenting opportunities. Four were identified:

- add a section on new technologies to the annual planning meetings, put pressure on each business to do something and encourage networking between the businesses;
- chair (or get his Finance Director or Strategy Director to chair) a co-ordination committee on new technologies;
- hire a consultant to evaluate the new technology potential for each business and then encourage the businesses to think long term;
- create a central department run by an internal or external champion to control development projects.

The CEO decided to add a section on new technologies to the planning process, but he felt this intervention alone did not involve enough co-ordination between the businesses. He felt that the co-ordination benefits would be particularly large in the early years (shared learning and shared experimentation costs), but because of the parenting opportunities he had identified, he feared that the businesses would want to work on their own before exposing their efforts to a wider group. He therefore set about evaluating the other three options (Exhibit 6.5).

Exhibit 6.5 Evaluating intervention options.

	Co-ordination	Consultant	Central department
Impact on parenting opportunity	Worst	Middle	Best
Ease of implementation	Middle	Best	Middle
Knock-on effects	Best	Middle	Worst

Each of the three options had strengths and weaknesses. A central department would be the best way to address the parenting opportunities because it would centralise evaluation decisions, overcome resistance to co-ordination and avoid the skill shortages. A co-ordination committee would be unlikely to address the evaluation or motivation biases, would not solve the skill shortages and might foster even more resistance to co-ordination.

The consultant solution would be the easiest to implement: the chief executive had good relations with a suitable firm who had worked with the company on previous occasions. A central department could be risky because it might be hard to find an appropriate individual and centralisation might be resisted by the businesses. A co-ordination committee would also have implementation problems because three businesses would not have skilled individuals to sit on the committee.

As far as knock-on effects were concerned, the co-ordination committee looked the best: it would be unlikely to cause contamination; it would not interfere with other parenting; it would be unlikely to demotivate or hurt innovativeness; and it would be supportive of the organisational philosophy of decentralisation and empowerment. A central function would have the danger of contamination from a one-solution-fits-all approach; might reduce motivation; and, in particular, might cause the businesses to abdicate any further responsibility for new technologies to the centre. Moreover, it would not fit well with the philosophy of decentralisation.

The net result of the evaluation was a marginal score in favour of the consultant route. However, the CEO was not satisfied. He wanted to find an intervention that would score 'best' on all three criteria. This caused some creative thinking about combining and sequencing interventions.

This led to the following plan, which was judged as scoring 'best' on all three criteria.

- Setting up a co-ordination group consisting of the two businesses with appropriate skills and an outside consultant. The CEO to attend some of these meetings.
- Financing a study by the consultant designed to help these two businesses and asking whether the other businesses would also like to be included.
- The consultant to report back to the group of four businesses supporting the project (the other businesses to be invited to 'attend').
- The CEO to use the recommendations from the consultant to persuade most of the businesses to upgrade their new technology skills and to share in two further projects:
  - a data collection and data 'mining' project to learn about how to exploit customer data;
  - an internet retailing project, in joint venture with another independent retailer, introduced to them by the consultant.
- In the longer term, the CEO to set up a central department to help lead technology development.

At the time of writing the plan has gone well. Four businesses agreed to support the consultant's work and the fifth attended the final report. Two additional projects have been launched, supported by four of the businesses (one of which had to be pressured into it). The fifth business is still not involved. The second phase projects are progressing well, and the CEO believes he is making good progress. He believes that more centralisation will be needed if he is to gain a big advantage over competitors, but he recognises that the risk of knock-on effects is still too high. These, he hopes, will reduce as the businesses gain more experience with the technologies. Hence he is planning to raise the issue of a central department in a year's time.

Summary

The decision flow chart (Exhibit 6.1) is a tool for helping managers decide what to do. It is also a useful framework for summarising the main messages of this book.

The four mental disciplines will help managers avoid the frustrations caused by the four mental biases. But the mental disciplines on their own are not enough to support a decision on what to do. They need to be harnessed to a decision process, which can be either intuitive or structured. The decision flow chart is our suggestion for a structured process, but we recognise that many managers will prefer to reach their decisions using a more intuitive approach. The structured process is particularly useful if managers are uncertain of their judgements, if they need to explain the judgements they have made, or if the decision is a joint one involving agreement between a number of managers.

Parent managers face a choice between doing nothing, choosing an exploratory approach and choosing an intervention designed to release some specified benefits. Our recommendations are clear:

• Do nothing if there is no parenting opportunity or if the benefit is small. (There are some exceptions to the small benefits rule explained on pages 142–7).
• Choose an exploratory intervention if the parenting opportunity or prize are unclear.

• Intervene decisively if the net benefit is clear and the parenting opportunity well understood.

We place particular emphasis on the first two, because they are often overlooked. Choosing not to intervene or to intervene only in exploratory mode is often the wisest course. Managers, impatient to make things happen, may feel uncomfortable with this advice, but the evidence of the mental disciplines and the decision flow chart should not be ignored: there are as many situations where the best choice is to do nothing or explore further as where decisive intervention is necessary.

Once a decision has been made to intervene decisively, parent managers need to decide how. We have suggested they identify three possible interventions, which can then be evaluated against each other. This is an important step because many decisions show a surprising lack of creativity. Managers are often reluctant to look beyond their first thought. The process of generating three options encourages a wider view without making the evaluation step too cumbersome.

In the final analysis, however, consider our flow chart as a memory jogger. Use it as a reference; use it together with more intuitive processes to stimulate thought; use it post hoc, to provide a rationale for an intuitive judgement already made; or, if you wish, use it systematically to work through the options for a difficult decision.

Our advice in these first six chapters is therefore essentially simple. There are four mental disciplines, four ways of looking at issues, that will help parent managers think clearly. There are some tools of analysis that help support these mental disciplines and help with the tough final choice about what intervention to make. None of this is rocket science or requires sophisticated analysis. It is all about clear thinking.

7

Taking Stock: How Well Is Your Approach to Synergy Working?

Some companies will benefit from a general review of their approach to synergy. This involves

- identifying the main areas of synergy potential and their likely impact on performance
- documenting the current approach to synergy, including its status in the overall corporate strategy
- judging the effectiveness of the current approach in releasing the synergies
- drawing up an agenda for change in organisation, strategy and mechanisms, including developing a list of links that need to be created.

Reviewing a company's overall approach is a major task and may not be worth the effort unless there are clear signals that change is needed.

In previous chapters, we have focused on how parent managers can choose better interventions to obtain specific synergy benefits. Sometimes, however, the parent has a broader agenda. The question is less: 'What should we do to target this particular benefit more effectively?' and more: 'Are there some important benefits that we are missing?' or 'Is there anything basically wrong with our whole approach to synergy management?'. In this chapter, we therefore set out a framework for corporate parents who wish to take stock of the overall effectiveness of their approach to synergies.

A review of synergy management can be triggered in a number of ways. A parent manager may suspect that co-ordination opportunities are being missed, but may not be sure what is being missed, how important it is, or what to do about it. A new chief executive may sense that his predecessor's emphasis on decentralisation has led unit managers to overlook sharing opportunities. A visit to other companies that sing the praises of co-ordination may raise concerns about what is being missed. Critical press comments about the company's failure to achieve synergies across its portfolio may prompt questions about what more could be achieved. Given our concern about 'synergy bias', we counsel caution in following up vague disquiets. But an audit of how well synergy management is working can be a useful step in allaying fears or pinpointing areas that need to be addressed.

A review can also be triggered by grumbles at lower levels in the company that current co-ordination efforts are pointless or damaging or contradictory. Business managers may complain that short-term budget targets prevent them from exploring potentially valuable synergy opportunities or about the pointlessness of corporate-wide conferences at expensive resorts to promote 'family feeling'. Corridor gossip about the negative influence of the parent may percolate up to the chief executive. More direct complaints may be received from frustrated business managers. Bottom-up pressures to think again about a company's approach to synergies should be taken seriously, and, if there are widespread or deep-seated concerns, a systematic and objective stock-taking may be in order.

Some companies build a periodic review of their cross-company initiatives into their regular planning processes. We are less enthusiastic about this practice, since it can easily lead either to superficial, year-by-year reiteration of what everyone already knows about the areas of overlap between businesses or to vain attempts to come up with new ideas. Unless there is a particular reason to review linkage management, it will probably cause more frustration than enlightenment. On the whole, therefore, we believe that a review should only be undertaken when there are identifiable reasons for doing so.

Good reasons to take stock of the current approach include:

- a belief that a major category of synergies such as international rationalisation, sharing technical know-how or joint development of new business opportunities, is being systematically missed;
- visible and costly failures of several recent synergy initiatives;
- evidence that business units are favouring links with third parties in preference to internal links.

While it would be useful to have a way of objectively deciding when a stock take is necessary, our experience suggests that it is best judged subjectively by thinking about how well the current organisation is working.

The purpose of a review should be to decide whether changes are needed in the overall corporate approach to synergies; to identify any specific opportunities that merit closer investigation; and to propose possible new linkage mechanisms or interventions.

A framework for a review

Our review framework is shown in Exhibit 7.1. It involves taking stock of both the synergy opportunities available and the current corporate approach to cross-company linkages. The effectiveness of the approach can be assessed by testing how well it fits with the opportunities. The assessment can then be used to pinpoint new initiatives that may be worth considering. The framework will bring out aspects of the overall approach that are working well or badly, and lead to proposals for changes.

Exhibit 7.1   Reviewing synergy parenting.

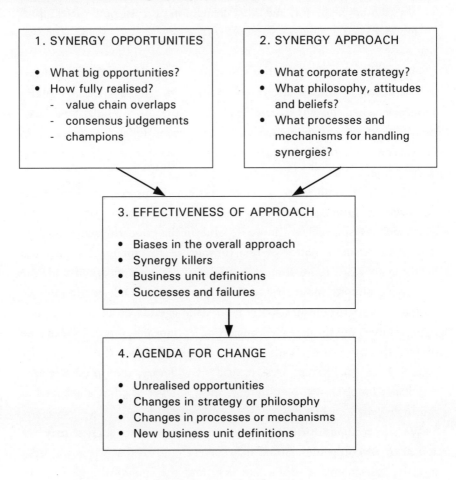

The value of the framework is that it obliges companies to address some fundamental questions:

- What is our current attitude to co-ordination between our business units, and how do we go about managing it?
- What do we believe are the main synergy opportunities in our portfolio, and how fully are we grasping them?
- How well suited is our current approach, including structures, processes and staff support, to the opportunities we believe are on offer?

• What current synergy initiatives should we drop, what new opportunities should we go for, and what changes in processes and mechanisms should we consider?

These questions can be asked of the whole company or of a multi-business division within a larger company. The framework is equally applicable when applied to any level above that of the individual business unit. However, when working at a division level, it is valuable to understand some of the broader corporate context in which the division is operating.

Although the framework provides a systematic means of tackling these questions, it should not be treated either as a straitjacket or a panacea. The emphasis of a review should depend on the concerns that prompted it. Is it primarily a matter of fine-tuning the current mechanisms and processes to work more smoothly, or are we more concerned with the underlying philosophy or structure of the company? Did we get into the review to beat the bushes to create a wide agenda of all possible new opportunities, or was it really a means of legitimising a fresh look at one or two specific issues? With different motivations for the review, the weight given to different areas of analysis will vary, the order in which activities take place will be different, and the level of effort and speed of the review will change.

We also recognise that the structured framework we suggest may not appeal to all companies. Some may have a culture that stresses a more intuitive assessment of issues, and may find the analytical approach we propose too constraining. Others may have their own preferred analyses that we have not included in our framework. We recognise that our approach is not the only way to undertake a review of linkage parenting, and we advise each company to tailor its approach to its own needs, culture and preferences.

As we discuss the different steps in the framework, readers should accordingly view our proposals as building blocks from which to construct their own review process, rather than as an inflexible 'how to do it' manual. We have found the steps useful in our work with companies, but we are not dogmatic about the framework we put forward.

Synergy opportunities

The first step in the review involves developing a list of major synergy opportunities and judging how fully they are being realised. The purpose is to unearth any important opportunities that are not currently being successfully grasped. This may prompt ideas for changes in the overall approach or for specific new interventions.

We have found that the checklist of types of synergy benefits given in Chapter 1 (page 4) can help managers to focus on opportunities that they would otherwise have overlooked. This check list classifies synergies under six headings: shared know-how, shared tangible resources, pooled negotiating power, co-ordinated strategies, vertical integration and combined new business creation.

While this checklist is not the only way in which synergy benefits can be classified, it provides a systematic way to flag up the vast majority of co-ordination initiatives.

The advantage of the classification is that it can trigger fresh thinking. Have we been too focussed on sharing know-how and tangible resources, and failed to think enough about ways in which we could co-ordinate the strategies of different businesses? Has pooled negotiating power been given the attention it deserves? Are there vertical integration links that we could manage better? The checklist helps to prevent systematic blind spots, for example consistent neglect of combined new business creation, and makes it more likely that the review of opportunities will be comprehensive.

In Chapters 2 and 3, we laid out our advice on how to define and size synergy opportunities and on how to assess the role that the parent should play in addressing them. Our message was that precision about the nature of the benefits, together with a clear understanding of the parenting opportunity, were needed. Before deciding on new parenting interventions, we argued, detailed analysis was essential.

But to undertake detailed analysis for every linkage opportunity as part of a general review is clearly not feasible. It would take too long and cost too much. The challenge is to find efficient ways of homing in quickly on possible areas of high unexploited potential.

In our research, we have identified three useful prompts that can help to reveal neglected potential: rough modelling of value chain overlaps; interviews, focus groups or questionnaires designed to draw out consensus from business unit and parent managers; and identification of pet projects or initiatives that are being strongly championed by individual managers.

Value chain overlaps

Businesses with value chains that overlap, or could overlap, are obvious candidates for linkage opportunities. If two businesses purchase similar components, what benefits might be available by co-ordinating their purchases? If two businesses have overseas offices in the same country, what could be saved by sharing premises, salesforces, or management? We have found that rough modelling of the extent of overlaps and of the economies of scale or utilisation available from sharing can rapidly yield a broad sizing of the benefits available in different areas. For example, a retail group was able to prioritise opportunities for joint purchasing by assessing the extent of overlaps in different product ranges between two of their chains, and estimating the level of extra purchase discounts that would be available from combined buying. Back-of-the-envelope calculations showed that there were only two product ranges with significant overlaps and, thus, real prospects for achieving better terms. More detailed analysis then focussed on these prime candidates. Although there was nothing precise or sophisticated about the modelling that led to this conclusion, it was highly effective in narrowing down the opportunities to consider.

Even rough value chain modelling can, however, be hard to do or too time consuming at the review stage. The benefits may not yet be sufficiently well-defined, or may be made up of several different component parts, or may be too numerous to analyse. An alternative is to rely on consensus judgements of informed managers.

Consensus judgements

When experienced managers agree that there is probably a worthwhile benefit to go for, their views deserve to be heard. If most of the marketing managers in different countries believe that they could benefit from sharing best practice in advertising, it is almost certainly worth trying to understand more about the opportunity. If, on the other hand, the corporate marketing director has suggested more sharing but the national marketing managers are lukewarm, it should probably be put on the backburner – at least unless the corporate director can argue convincingly that the national managers may be misjudging the opportunity. In the difficult field of synergies, the gut-feel and intuitive judgement of experienced managers should carry considerable weight.

In companies where information flows freely and managers are encouraged to express their views, it is comparatively easy for parent managers to discern an emerging consensus. In other companies, it can be much more difficult. Managers from different units may not meet together often enough to share views, or may not feel empowered to express their views to each other. They may also be constrained to follow prevailing corporate policies rather than challenge them. Whatever the reason, a structured approach to eliciting the consensus is frequently needed.

There are a variety of ways to draw out consensus judgements, ranging from questionnaires, through focus groups, to some form of systematic interviewing process. The method chosen needs to be tailored to the circumstances of the company – and we have adopted somewhat different methods in each of the companies we have worked with. In all cases, however, the objective is to discover whether informed managers generally feel that there are important unexplored opportunities going begging, and, if so, what priorities they should receive. In the sidebar – 'Identifying unrealised synergy opportunities in Consco' – we describe the approach taken at a company that we shall call 'Consco'. We will use Consco as an illustrative example throughout this chapter.

Identifying unrealised synergy opportunities in Consco

Consco is a multinational consumer goods company, with operations in 65 countries worldwide. The company decided to undertake an audit of its synergy parenting, focused on the 22 national operating companies in Europe. These units varied in size and sophistication from large, well-established operations in countries such as Germany and the UK, through medium-sized companies in countries such as Denmark and Spain, to new, developing units in the countries of Eastern Europe. Local tastes, channels of distribution and market conditions varied throughout Europe, but there was a trend to increasing uniformity, which Consco was encouraging through the promotion of major international brands.

To determine whether managers in Consco generally believed that there were unrealised co-ordination opportunities, it used a questionnaire survey, followed up with focus-group discussions. The survey allowed managers to give their judgements concerning both the potential size (rated on a four-point scale) of different opportunities and the extent to which the benefit was being realised (% currently achieved). From pilot interviews, 22 opportunity areas, covering shared marketing know-how, strategy and policy co-ordination, and supply chain management emerged for consideration. The supply chain area contained a mix of opportunities, including shared know-how, shared tangible resources and pooled negotiating power.

The results of this analysis are shown in exhibit 7.2. The precise numerical results are less important than the fact that there appears to be a consensus on several areas of high unrealized potential, including purchasing co-ordination, co-ordination of relationships with certain key customers, and best-practice sharing in training and management development. Some areas of marketing tactics and product-range co-ordination also appear to represent large but better realised opportunities. In the focus-group discussions, it was possible to determine why managers felt that there was unrealised potential in these areas, and to explore what could be done about it.

The value of the survey and the focus groups lay in allowing managers time to reflect and share their views about these synergy opportunities. While there was by no means unanimity, most managers were surprised to discover how many of their colleagues shared similar views about a number of the opportunities. Whereas there had previously been uncertainty about whether it was really worth devoting more effort to these issues, the audit helped convince parent and business managers that they were leaving money on the table and therefore needed to take some action.

Exhibit 7.2   Synergy opportunities in Consco.

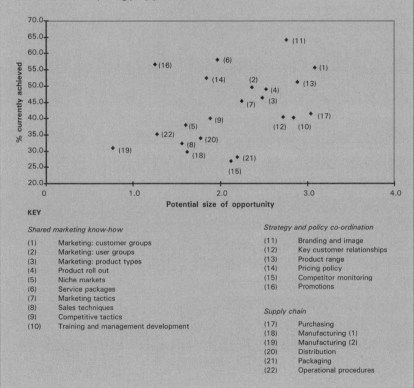

KEY

Shared marketing know-how

(1)   Marketing: customer groups
(2)   Marketing: user groups
(3)   Marketing: product types
(4)   Product roll out
(5)   Niche markets
(6)   Service packages
(7)   Marketing tactics
(8)   Sales techniques
(9)   Competitive tactics
(10)   Training and management development

Strategy and policy co-ordination

(11)   Branding and image
(12)   Key customer relationships
(13)   Product range
(14)   Pricing policy
(15)   Competitor monitoring
(16)   Promotions

Supply chain

(17)   Purchasing
(18)   Manufacturing (1)
(19)   Manufacturing (2)
(20)   Distribution
(21)   Packaging
(22)   Operational procedures

Championing

A third valuable prompt comes from championing. We have already argued in Chapter 4 that strong and enthusiastic champions are important for the effective implementation of new interventions. We believe that they can also provide a short cut to identifying priority opportunity areas. If a manager feels so powerfully that an opportunity is worthwhile that he is willing to lobby for it, devote personal sweat equity to it, and risk the displeasure of his colleagues and bosses by repeatedly advocating it, it is usually worth taking notice.

There is little danger that strong champions will not be heard by the corporate parent. The danger is more that they will be too readily discounted. Persistent champions, particularly if their ideas challenge vested interests, can face strong opposition. Their views may be dismissed as unrealistic or irrelevant, or they may be labelled eccentrics or troublemakers. Prudent managers then pipe down, and learn to live with their frustrations. However, frustrated champions welcome any chance to promote their pet projects. A review of linkage parenting is a good opportunity to give them an objective hearing. Our advice is to listen carefully to what they have to say – even if the rest of the organisation has long ago decided not to.

Creativity and realism

In drawing up the shortlist of opportunities that merit detailed consideration, we need to balance creativity and open-mindedness with realism. We want managers with new ideas to come forward, we want to encourage brainstorming that will generate fresh thinking, we want to give a hearing to highly motivated champions. Especially if the purpose of the review is to make sure we're not missing something, we should be positive about new suggestions and supportive of 'thinking the unthinkable'.

We should also be willing to accept that some promising ideas may be clouded by considerable uncertainty. In Consco, for example, there was widespread support for more sharing of best practice in training and management development. But the benefits available were somewhat nebulous. Some managers had fairly specific ideas about how course designs or materials could be shared better. Others were simply reflecting a sense that this was an increasingly important area, in which they did not feel that their units were doing a very good job. Some had anecdotes or examples to support their views. But there was considerable uncertainty about where the real opportunities lay and how they should be pursued. And, in some situations, there is intrinsic uncertainty about the nature of the benefits. In businesses in the middle of rapid technological change, such as media and communications, the benefits of collaborating to develop new businesses to some extent depend on market and technology developments that are simply not predictable. The review should encourage managers to put forward speculative or uncertain opportunities: on closer examination they may turn out to contain real nuggets of gold. But any interventions to pursue them will probably have to be exploratory, designed to find out whether there are solid benefits to be obtained or not.

In creating a short-list of ideas to examine more closely, we should, however, guard against pursuing mirages, and question whether there really are likely to be parenting opportunities to address. When we assess the shortlisted ideas, we shall need to be rigorous in applying the mental disciplines to them. In drawing up the short-list, we should therefore reject ideas if there is insufficient logic or evidence to support them. For example, if the champion of a shared salesforce appears to have given little serious consideration to important details, such as salesmen's calling patterns or the purchase criteria of customers, his proposal should receive less weight. Or if, on reflection, no-one can see any possible parenting opportunities associated with the targeted benefit, we should avoid wasting time with further investigation of it. We need to blend support for fresh thinking with the reality checks and tough-mindedness that the mental disciplines provide. It is the ideas that will stand up under closer analysis that we are interested in.

Synergy approach

The next step in the review is to lay out the main features of the company's approach to synergy management. It should cover the role that synergies play within the corporate strategy. It should bring out the company's underlying philosophy, attitudes and beliefs concerning the units' relationships to each other and to the centre. And it should make explicit the mechanisms and processes that the company typically uses to deal with these issues.

Corporate strategy

In our research on corporate strategy, we have found that different companies place very different emphases on the horizontal and vertical linkages that they foster. Some companies, such as Hanson (before the breakup), Emerson, RTZ and BTR (prior to 1995), place much more weight on the value that they add through stand-alone parenting (See Chapter 5) than through linkage parenting. Others, such as Banc One, Unilever, 3M, ABB and Canon, have always seen the management of synergies as a key part of their corporate strategies.[1] Business managers in organisations such as Hanson know that the main focus of the parent's attention will be on opportunities to improve the performance of each business as a stand-alone entity, and that they will receive few brownie points for collaborative efforts with other units. By contrast, business managers in Canon or Unilever know that their bosses expect and require them to seek out and participate in opportunities for working together with other units. Furthermore, they know what sorts of synergies the parent typically promotes most energetically. In Canon, for example, the strongest drive is for new product developments that require co-operation across business unit boundaries, while in Unilever the transfer of product and market information across geographic boundaries is critical.

Exhibit 7.3 summarises the main sources of value creation identified in one international manufacturing and marketing company. This way of summarising the corporate strategy into a list of parenting tasks helps position the importance of synergy initiatives versus other forms of parenting.

Exhibit 7.3   Sources of parenting value creation in a consumer products company (in order of size of potential value added).

- Transferring know-how about products, markets, marketing, manufacturing and other functions from/to business units around the world.
- Helping businesses (mainly in developed economies) avoid the pitfall of under investment in new product development and consumer understanding.
- Creating a value-based performance culture that has low tolerance of unnecessary costs or weak performance, yet is capable of investing where necessary.
- Orchestrating pools of mobile management talent so that businesses can draw on them in times of need.
- Developing and appointing outstanding managers to lead each business, with skills appropriate to the particular challenges of that business.
- Helping businesses (mainly in emerging markets) to avoid common pitfalls, such as insufficient investment in local management or poor timing of major commitments.
- Developing valuable relationships with potential partners and influential governments, and building the company brand into one of the world's leading corporate brands.
- Providing cost effective central services and corporate governance activities.

In summary, the review should document the priority given to linkage issues versus other forms of parenting and record the types of linkages that feature most prominently as key sources of added value. The review should also record the direction of movement in the corporate strategy. Is the company looking to build more synergies in the future or unwind some of the links and co-ordinated activities that currently exist? The current corporate strategy and the perceived direction of movement influences the sort of synergies that managers are likely to pursue and the priority they give them.

Philosophy, attitudes and beliefs

Companies also have different underlying attitudes and beliefs about how best to handle linkages. Often these differences concern the advantages of centralisation or decentralisation. To achieve benefits from pooled purchasing power, for example, a parent with a belief in the efficacy of central initiatives may set up a central purchasing department and insist that all purchases of certain items are handled by this department. Conversely, a parent that favours decentralised networking may simply circulate data on the purchasing terms and conditions being achieved by each unit, maintaining strong pressure on the businesses to reduce their individual unit costs. Such an intervention leaves the businesses much freer to determine whether and how they wish to work with other businesses to improve their purchasing power, but gives them no direct help or guidance about what to do. Between these extremes, there are a variety of other possibilities, such as establishing joint purchasing teams with members from different businesses, nominating selected businesses to act as lead units in purchasing for different items, centralising certain aspects of negotiations on terms and conditions but allowing each business to make its own buying decisions, and hiring a central purchasing expert who is available to the businesses, but need only be used by them if they choose.

For any synergy benefit, a range of possible intervention options can be arrayed along a spectrum of more versus less centralist interventions (see Exhibit 7.4). Some companies, such as Mars and Unilever, are philosophically committed to the decentralised, networking end of the spectrum. They believe that it is vital to preserve business–unit autonomy and leave decisions to business–unit managements. Wary of central interference, they prefer to rely on the 'enlightened self-interest' of unit managers to guide linkages. Other companies, such as Canon or Rentokil, are more comfortable mandating policies or decisions from the centre on a range of issues. Although they accept the importance of unit motivation and initiative, they believe that there are many important benefits that will not be realised unless the parent makes the decisions.

Exhibit 7.4   Differences in linkage philosophy.

	Belief in decentralisation ———	Mixed ———	Belief in central direction
Know-how sharing	• Network facilitation	• Some central policies • Centres of excellence • Lead units • Franchise	• Mandatory central policies/directives
Tangible resources sharing	• Internal j.v.s./contracts • Voluntary use of shared resource units, set up as profit centres	• Limited central func- tions and resources • Service level agreements	• Mandatory central functions and resources • Incomplete SBUs
Pooled negotiating power	• Information sharing • Joint SBU teams and initiatives	• Lead units	• Central functions, experts
Vertical integration	• Third party trading relationships, but first refusal in-house	• Negotiated transfer prices • In-house preference • Centre influences relationship	• Centre sets transfer prices, and manages relationships for corporate benefit
Co-ordinated strategies	• Centre arbitrates • Minimal constraints on scope/strategy	• Restrained central role • Matrix structure • Task forces • Franchise	• Centre directs • Low SBU autonomy
New business creation	• SBU driven	• Task forces drawn from centre and SBUs	• Centrally driven

Differences in attitudes concerning the appropriate degree of centralisation affect the range of intervention options that a parent is likely to perceive. Those who favour decentralised solutions will tend to give little or no consideration to more mandatory central interventions. Those who typically mandate central policies and decisions will be less sensitive to how much can be accomplished through a variety of measures that encourage networking. Corporate linkage philosophies represent blinkers that constrain the options that receive attention.

Another important factor is the corporate parent's attitude to central staff resources. Should large, heavyweight staff groups be set up or not? Should the businesses be forced to work with the corporate staffs, or should their use by the businesses be voluntary? As with centralisation/ decentralisation choices, companies tend to have a dominant philosophy which governs the role of staff in managing linkages. Companies such as

ABB are strenuously opposed to the use of corporate staffs, wherever possible relying on decisions and resources in the business units. They fear that, lacking direct profit responsibility, staffs can easily lose touch with the needs of the businesses and take on a life of their own, in which power and empire-building take precedence over the benefits delivered to the corporation. Other companies, 3M or Cooper for instance, believe that corporate staffs, at least in selected areas, are the best way to ensure that specialist expertise is developed and shared among units. They are therefore a source of valuable linkages. These beliefs will be reflected in the synergy interventions that the parent makes.

Different philosophies therefore influence the sorts of synergies that will be pursued and the means which will be used to pursue them. Take, for example, a new product-development initiative involving joint work between two or more business units. At one extreme, a 'Hanson' approach, suspicious of shared responsibilities of this sort, would likely press for the initiative to be pursued within one of the businesses or else dropped. By contrast, a 'Unilever' approach would be to provide encouragement and, if necessary, expert assistance, while allowing the businesses to pursue the matter in their own way, within a framework of strong corporate cultural norms to guide decision-making. A 'Canon' approach would be different again, entailing willingness to give high corporate priority to the project, including assignment of numbers of both corporate and business staff to work full-time on the project to see it through to commercialisation. Some assessment of the underlying corporate attitudes and beliefs about linkages should therefore form part of the review.

Mechanisms and processes

Companies also differ in the nature of the specific mechanisms and processes that they typically use to manage co-ordination. The review should identify the mechanisms and processes that are most frequently used, and should articulate the impact that they have on synergy management. What is the nature and importance of the budget and planning processes, and how, if at all, do they affect cross-company initiatives? What sort of cross-business committees are in place and how do they work? What staff groups exist and what role do they play in linkages?

In Chapter 4, we argued that 'well-grooved' mechanisms are an important factor in gauging the ease with which a company's synergy interventions will be implemented. Equally, ineffective or ill-suited mechanisms and processes can account for failure to realise some opportunities.

'Five lenses analysis'

As a means of describing and analysing the parent's approach to synergy issues, we have found that a display that views the characteristics of the parent through five inter-linked lenses is useful[2] (see Exhibit 7.5). The five lenses are:

- The beliefs, knowledge or mental maps that guide the behaviour and decisions of senior managers in the parent organisation. These mental maps determine the corporate linkage strategy and philosophy, and guide the parent's thinking about the selection and implementation of linkage mechanisms and interventions.

- The structure of the company, including the way in which the business units are defined and the nature of parenting structures to which they report, and the systems and processes through which parent managers mainly exercise influence, pressure and control. The business-unit definitions determine what links between units need to be managed; the nature of the parenting structure, for example whether there are product divisions, geographical divisions, or a matrix structure, influences the parenting opportunities that will be pursued; and the systems and processes that are in place determine how they are most likely to be handled.

- The functional staffs, central service groups, and corporate resources that are important in synergy management. The size, composition and strengths of the corporate staff and the way in which they operate are key components of the overall approach to cross-company working.

- The people in the parent organisation. The experience, skills and biases of key individuals in the parent have a major impact on synergy management.

- The extent to which authority is delegated to business managers, together with the criteria by which their performance is judged and the rewards or sanctions for good or poor performance; we refer to this as the 'decentralisation contract' for each business. The manner in which decentralisation contracts are defined influences the sorts of linkage interventions that the parent is likely to make and that the businesses are likely to accept.

We have found that these five lenses provide a useful checklist for itemising those features of the corporate parent's approach to the management of synergies that matter most. By running through each of these headings and taking stock of the key features under each, a picture of the overall approach can be built up and made explicit. The five lenses can also be used to bring out ways in which the approach is changing, giving a direction of movement as well as a static picture.

In the sidebar – 'Consco's synergy parenting approach' – we have laid out a five-lenses description of the linkage parenting characteristics of Consco.

Exhibit 7.5 Parenting characteristics.

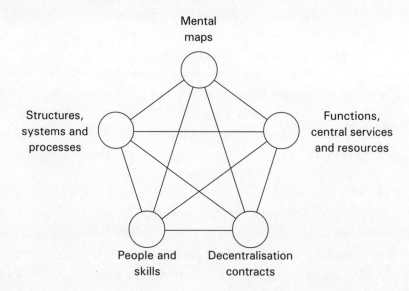

Consco's synergy parenting approach

Through in-depth interviews with about 15 managers, mainly from the corporate parent, and focus groups involving a further 30 managers, mainly from the operating units, a five lenses description of Consco's historical synergy parenting approach was developed (Exhibit 7.6).

Exhibit 7.6   Consco's synergy parenting.

- Local flexibility and responsiveness wins competitively
- Marketing and product innovation as csfs

- Geographical structure (national units/regions/centre)
- Budget as main management process

- Large corporate technical and marketing staffs
- Strong corporate brand

MM

S, S & P

Fn, S & R

P & S

DC

- Experienced and successful unit line managers
- Weak and low status staff managers

- Unit autonomy and responsibility
- Unit profitability as main performance measure

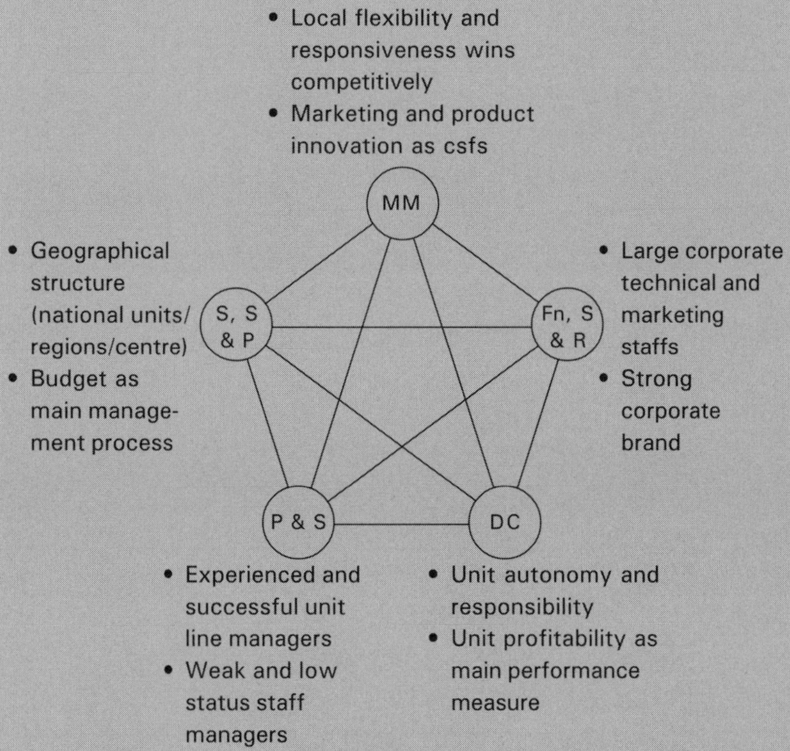

Consco's basic philosophy had always stressed unit autonomy and flexibility. National operating companies had been encouraged to develop their own products and marketing campaigns, taking account of local market differences. As a result, Consco prided itself on responding faster to local opportunities that its competitors. It was by this means that the company had been able to succeed against larger, better resourced, but more centralised rivals.

Several features of Consco's approach to synergy followed from this basic philosophy. Country managing directors were seen as key to success, and were strongly incentivised on the results achieved in their units. The national companies reported to four regional heads (Europe, the Americas, Asia-Pacific, and the Middle-East and Africa). The key management process was the annual budget, with tough negotiations over budget targets for each unit, close monitoring of results, and strong profit-based incentives for country managers. The importance of experienced, successful country managers, with good entrepreneurial instincts, was widely recognised.

There were quite extensive corporate technical and marketing staffs. The technical staffs worked on major product developments, though local companies were free to introduce their own modifications. The marketing staff issued guidelines to co-ordinate product positioning, pricing and marketing tactics, though, again, there was considerable local discretion over whether and how to follow the guidelines. There were also fairly strict policies on the use of the corporate brand, which was regarded as an important asset.

Aside from corporate technical and marketing guidelines, most co-ordination issues tended to be handled through dialogue between operating company managers and their regional bosses, or through informal one-to-one meetings between colleagues from the units. Given the high status of line managers relative to the corporate staff, line contacts or informal networking of this sort were usually the means of grasping synergy benefits rather than staff interventions.

Despite Consco's historical success, several managers at all levels felt that the increasing size and geographical spread of the company, coupled with shrinking local differences and increasing product-range harmonisation in Europe, called into question several features of the approach.

Effectiveness of approach

The third step is to assess the effectiveness of the current synergy approach. How well does the approach match up with the opportunities?

Is it working reasonably well, apart from a few specific problems? Are there any fundamental shortcomings that need to be tackled? Once the approach and the opportunities have been laid out in the first two steps of the review, the answers to these questions may be readily apparent. There are, however, some more structured questions that it may be useful to ask. These include:

- Are there biases in the overall approach that condition which opportunities will be realised?
- Are there any aspects of the approach which are impeding linkages; are there any 'synergy killers'?
- Do any business unit definitions need to be changed?
- What have been the successes and failures of the approach, and what problems need addressing?

Biases in the overall approach

Earlier in this chapter, we contrasted the corporate strategies and philosophies of different companies, including Hanson, Unilever, ABB and Canon. The differences in these companies' approaches to synergies mean that they will each steer away from certain sorts of interventions and towards others: their approaches bias both the types of linkages they are likely to emphasise and the means by which they will be pursued.

Nearly all companies have biases in their linkage parenting, and a value of the review is to lay out what they are. What does the corporate strategy emphasise? What are the dominant mental maps that are driving the linkage interventions that the parent chooses to make? What are the well-grooved processes that are usually chosen as the preferred way to intervene? If we can make these biases explicit, we may be able to see why certain synergy opportunities are grasped, while others are systematically overlooked; why some initiatives run smoothly, while others are always contentious and difficult.

● In one manufacturer of automotive components, the corporate strategy stressed the importance of global co-ordination across different national companies. This strategy led to cost savings and superior customer service in many areas. However, it also led to pressure for rationalisation of the product range that carried high opportunity costs in some countries. The basic presumption in favour of international co-ordination made it very difficult for the countries in question to get a fair hearing on these costs. Instead, they were accused of NIH thinking and told to fall into line with global policy. The bias in favour of international co-ordination in the corporate strategy prevented the parent from taking a balanced view of the advantages and disadvantages of product-range rationalisation.

● In a building products company, there was a strong commitment to decentralised networking as the best way to capture synergies, based partly on history and partly on a belief in the need to respect differences in each business unit's markets. When the corporate parent wanted to encourage all the businesses to adopt a common MIS system, the networking bias resulted in an endless sequence of project-team meetings, in which it was impossible to reach agreement on a new standard system for all the businesses. It was only after literally years of delay that the parent insisted on a choice being made and pushed it through. The bias in favour of networking prevented a stronger corporate lead from being taken earlier.

The biases in a company's overall approach will make it specially effective at handling certain sorts of linkages, but ineffective at others. For example, in Chapter 3 we showed that there are some parenting opportunities that require mandated central decisions and are unlikely to be grasped through interventions that simply aim to promote networking between the businesses. Hence, a parent with a bias in favour of decentralised networking is unlikely to be successful at realising these sorts of parenting opportunities. Similarly, a staff-averse company that always tends to use cross-business project teams to handle linkages will find it difficult to push through parenting opportunities for which central staffs are needed. By making explicit any biases in the approach, we may be able to understand better why some opportunities are being successfully realised while others are proving problematic. We can then decide whether to maintain the approach and endorse its biases or to consider making changes.

In the sidebar – 'Effectiveness of Consco's synergy parenting' – we show how the biases in Consco's approach were affecting the opportunities they were able to pursue.

Synergy killers

Most of this book – and most discussions of synergy – concern ways in which the corporate parent can make linkages between business units work better. Unfortunately, the harsh reality is that the corporate parent often inadvertently makes these connections more difficult, not easier. We need to recognise this fact, and can use a review of linkage parenting as a means of rooting out things that are impeding linkages. We refer to policies or characteristics of the parent that are systematically inhibiting linkages as 'synergy killers'.

The effectiveness of the approach to linkages will be compromised if any of the following synergy killers are present:

• *Inhibiting corporate strategy.* The most common way in which the corporate-level strategy can work against synergy is through lack of clarity. Lack of clarity about corporate priorities leads managers to be excessively cautious about when they collaborate and with whom. If managers in the businesses are unsure whether the corporate parent expects them to be co-ordinating their technical efforts or looking for cost savings in marketing, the uncertainty can leave them paralysed. A more obvious, if rarer, problem stems from corporate strategies that actively discourage linkages of any sort. In a notorious memorandum written after GEC's acquisition of English Electric, Lord Weinstock informed the managers of the English Electric businesses that all cross-unit committees and projects were to be disbanded forthwith. In future, they would have only one responsibility: the performance of their own units. Though few companies today take such a radical stance against synergies between businesses, some corporate-level strategies still discourage co-operation. 'In my view', stated one chief executive, 'synergy is always an illusion. What is more, it fatally damages accountability'. Not surprisingly, this attitude had a dampening effect on unit managers' attempts to work together.

- *Infighting between the barons.* In some companies, there are battles raging between senior managers. The battles may be about differences in corporate strategy or management philosophy. They may be about competition between managers for the top job. They may be due to personality clashes. They may be due to previous collaborations where one party felt let down. Whatever the reason, these battles have a huge negative impact on co-operation. Managers lower down are often aware of lost opportunities, but the climate of hostility between their bosses means that co-operation to pursue them is stifled. It is simply not acceptable to be seen to be 'working with the enemy'.

- *Culture of secrecy.* In secretive companies, people play their cards close to their chests. Information about business unit performance, new product plans, operating issues, and organisation structures is given out reluctantly. In these circumstances, co-operation is hard, not only because it is difficult to find out what is going on in other units, but also because the free flow of information and communication that is needed to oil the wheels of synergies is inhibited. Why do these cultures occur? Sometimes it is fear of competitor espionage. Sometimes it is a result of resisting corporate information requests and interference. Sometimes it is associated with baronial infighting. Whatever the cause, a culture of secrecy reduces synergy.

- *Misaligned incentives.* In many companies, bonus systems and promotion criteria depend largely or exclusively on the results managers achieve in their own businesses, and give no credit for contributions to other businesses or the corporate whole. The personal incentive system then makes it more difficult for business managers to co-operate, unless they can structure a deal that rewards all the units involved. Where the synergy involves a sacrifice by one unit to help others, and there is no ready process by which to compensate the loser, the incentive system will block progress. Again and again, we encountered situations in which this prevented managers from helping colleagues in other businesses, even though there was a clear net benefit. Where win/lose trade-offs exist, reward systems should aim to make it easier for business managers to co-operate; all too often, they have precisely the reverse effect.

- *Excessive performance pressure.* When managers are hounded by close-to-impossible targets, they are apt to become defensive and inward-looking. In companies where business unit performance is paramount and where targets are set too high, managers often concentrate exclusively on things within their own immediate control and cease to be comfortable with situations where they must rely on their colleagues' co-operation. Oppressive targets damp down the spirit of mutuality and collaboration from which synergies flow.

- *Insulation from performance pressure.* At the opposite end of the spectrum from excessive performance pressure is insulation from performance pressure. If business units are insulated from performance pressures, the basic drive of enlightened self-interest, on which so many beneficial sharing initiatives depend, will be weakened. In companies where synergies thrive, such as Mars or Canon, senior managers keep up the pressure for constant improvement, knowing that this leads to more energy and creativity in seeking out ways in which the businesses can benefit from working together. In companies where the parent insulates the businesses from such pressures, the businesses are less likely to seek out mutually rewarding synergies.

- *Domineering corporate staff.* If corporate staff groups have domineering or insensitive attitudes, business managers will automatically reject their ideas for improving linkages, however sound they may be. In a major chemical company with old-established functional baronies, the heads of the corporate staff departments were inclined to issue policies and guidelines to the businesses with little consultation or recognition of inter-company differences. Over time, the business heads became adept at passive resistance and nonco-operation, spending much more time on the tactics of opposition than on assessing whether the proposed policies were, in fact, beneficial. As a result, genuine synergy opportunities were resisted as strenuously as misguided attempts at standardisation.

- *Mistrust.* An atmosphere of mistrust undermines co-operation. If the businesses believe that their sister units are out to take advantage of them, or are always unwilling to put themselves out to help, relations are quickly soured to the point where even well-intentioned initiatives are blocked. Equally, if a climate of opinion has grown up where business managers believe that corporate management or staff are incompetent or untrustworthy, synergy interventions are likely to be resisted in principle. Expensive, high profile failures seriously undermine the credibility and prospects of any future proposal. Particular problems arise when the parent is suspected of having a hidden agenda, since all initiatives will be scrutinized for ulterior motives, and interpreted in the worst possible light.

All companies have some synergy killers. Our concern should be with pathological characteristics that may be causing widespread damage, not with minor irritants. Is there a strong sense that some of the parent's characteristics are really preventing collaboration? Can we see evidence from the unrealised opportunities that indicates that these synergy killers are having a real impact? How can the parent adjust the corporate context to make linkages work better? In the Consco example, the two major synergy killers that needed to be tackled were the bonus system and the low regard for corporate staffs.

While synergy killers inhibit linkages, their opposites create the sort of fertile ground in which co-operation flourishes. Clear corporate strategies that support high priority synergies; good personal relationships between senior managers in the businesses; an open culture that promotes sharing; incentive systems that reward attempts to create synergies; corporate pressure to raise performance through sharing best practices; competent staff units that are sensitive in their relationships with the businesses; and an atmosphere of mutual trust and support are all conducive to perceiving synergy opportunities and implementing them successfully. The parent should aim to nurture synergies through creating these fertile ground conditions. Hence, even if no real synergy killers exist, the review may still pinpoint ways in which the corporate context could be made more fertile for synergies.

Business unit definitions

The boundaries established around a group's business units are fundamental for the approach to synergies. By changing the definition of the
business units, the parent automatically changes the nature of the potential links between business units. If a new European unit is set up out of
previously separate national units, issues of manufacturing co-ordination
that used to be handled as linkages between separate units are now managed within a single larger entity. 'Internalising' the linkages in this way
makes a big difference, because there is now a single general manager
for the combined business who is in a position to decide on trade-offs
between the sub-units and who will be held responsible for the results
of the integrated entity. This makes certain interventions much easier to
push through, although it may involve some reduction in focus on the
product-market niches within the larger entity.

The trade-offs between breadth and focus in business-unit definition
are complex, and go well beyond the scope of this book. There are,
however, some business-unit definition issues that should be addressed
in a review of synergy management. In particular, it is important to raise
the following questions:

• Are there some important synergies that are never likely to be realised
  with the current business unit definitions? If so, are there alternative
  definitions that should be considered?
• Are certain synergies harder to achieve because of the manner in which
  the boundaries around the business units are set up and managed?

There are some circumstances in which co-ordination between separate
businesses is never likely to be achieved, however beneficial it may be
for the group. If, for example, the collective net benefits involve costs to
one or more units that are hard or impossible to compensate for, the
initiative is likely to be blocked. Thus, it may be almost impossible to
bring about co-ordinated production planning between separate units if
it involves one or more units shutting their factories and transferring
production to another. To avoid the consequent reduction in power and
status, the general managers of the units in question will be likely to go

to any lengths to block or undermine the initiative. Conclusion: the best way to achieve this synergy benefit will probably be to redefine the business to encompass all the previously separate units, giving responsibility for optimising performance to a single management team.

Other situations in which managers should consider a redefinition of the businesses to achieve desirable synergies include the following.

- Deeply embedded hostility and mistrust between senior managers in the different units. If the rivalry between the general managers of the units is intense, they may simply be unwilling to work together, whatever the benefits. The solution may be to redefine the business units and give responsibility for both of them to one or other of the managers.
- Hard-to-allocate costs and revenues. If shared production facilities or the lack of an open third-party market for products traded between the units make it difficult to agree a split of costs and revenues, any form of co-operation is likely to suffer, since underlying disputes about transfer prices and allocated costs will dominate everything else. In such circumstances, it is often better to expand the business definition to include both units, with a single bottom line. Co-ordination issues then become a means to maximise aggregate profitability rather than the pretext for haggling over how to divide up the results.
- Need for speedy and continuous resolution of trade-off judgements. Concerns about contamination (see Chapter 5) and lack of focus have led many companies to create more and more separate profit centres, each with its own management and strategy. This drive for business focus creates major difficulties if the separate businesses need to be in constant touch with each other and have to resolve a series of difficult day-to-day trade-offs. For example, if two petrochemical businesses share a process plant and continuous decisions about output mix are needed to achieve the optimum overall profitability, taking account of the shifting relative prices of different inputs and of different end products, the two businesses will be locked in constant complex negotiations about how to run the plant. A structure in which a single management team is responsible for optimising both businesses is likely to work more smoothly.

The underlying issue is whether, for whatever reason, co-ordination between the separate businesses' management teams will always be much less effective than co-ordination under a single management team. Managers should therefore examine the current business-unit boundaries to see if they are preventing any important synergies from taking place. If they are, consider altering the boundaries.

Judgements about whether a redefinition of the businesses is necessary should also reflect the nature of the boundaries. If decentralisation contracts emphasise the autonomy of the business heads and provide few incentives or opportunities for them to work together, potential problems resulting from separate business definitions will be magnified. If, however, business heads do not expect to have full control over all the functions and resources they need in their businesses, and work in a context that encourages and requires frequent liaison with colleagues from other businesses and from central functions, the boundaries around the separate businesses will be more naturally permeable. In Canon, for example, business managers are very ready to work on cross-business project teams, to draw on corporate staff support, and to co-ordinate with other businesses: the corporate approach to co-ordination stresses the connections between the businesses, not the boundaries that separate them. With more permeable boundaries around the businesses, there is more flexibility to make different business definitions work well. With more separation between businesses, there is a greater premium on drawing the boundaries in ways that will internalise linkages that would otherwise become problematic.

Successes and failures

Last, but not least, the effectiveness of the overall approach can be tested in terms of evident successes and failures: well and poorly rated mechanisms and processes, fully and less fully realised synergy opportunities, patterns of success and failure that cast light on organisational strengths and weaknesses.

As part of the audit of the current approach, it is essential to canvas opinion about the effectiveness of the main systems and processes for managing synergies, and of the key staff groups that promote them. Surveys, in-depth discussions or focus groups can bring well-grooved and successful mechanisms into relief and pinpoint areas of friction or dissatisfaction. Poorly rated mechanisms should then be examined more carefully. What are the causes of dissatisfaction? Is it a mechanism for chasing mirages? Are the parenting opportunities on which it is targeted clear, or is it being driven by parenting bias? Is it wasting the time of managers at the centre or in the businesses? Should we consider other ways of intervening to realise the target benefits, or should we simply discontinue our efforts if they are not working?

Another way into the successes and failures analysis is via the synergy opportunities review. Do the unrealised opportunities indicate some underlying gap or shortcoming in our approach? Is there some mismatch between the processes or interventions we use for getting at the opportunities and the nature of the opportunities? If, for example, we are consistently failing to achieve the benefits of better capacity utilisation that vertical integration should provide, is this because there is something wrong with our transfer-pricing processes or with our approach to combined investment planning? Or are our business-specific performance measures to blame? Our quest should be to unearth new or different mechanisms for intervening that are better suited for the parenting opportunities open to us, in order to reduce the number of important unrealised opportunities.

We have also found that a retrospective analysis of patterns of success and failure with previous synergy interventions can be useful. Which synergies have we managed well – and probably taken for granted? What notorious initiatives have caused the most trouble and yielded the least benefit? What can we learn from these successes and failures?

By examining the successes, we will be able to see more clearly what mechanisms work best for us. What opportunities have we derived most benefit from? By what means did we realise these opportunities? Answers to these questions will reveal what the organisation's well-grooved mechanisms and processes are, and will help to shape thinking about how to tackle new opportunities. By examining the failures, we may discover underlying weaknesses in our skills or processes, or organisational blockages and synergy killers that lie behind our inability to implement certain types of synergies successfully. A sense of these underlying patterns is useful in assessing the effectiveness of the approach.

The sidebar – 'Effectiveness of Consco's synergy parenting' – summarises the strengths and weaknesses of Consco's synergy management.

Effectiveness of Consco's synergy parenting

Biases in the Approach

Consco's historical emphasis on decentralised operating company responsibilities meant that there was a strong bias in favour of networking between units as the preferred means of handling co-ordination. With certain exceptions (basic new product developments, brand protection policies), the corporate parent relied on good personal relationships between unit heads, catalysed by a performance-oriented culture, for the identification and pursuit of synergy opportunities.

As the range of issues on which co-ordination might be desirable and the number of operating units increased, the ability of the informal networking process to do justice to the opportunities available waned. Senior business-unit managers did not have enough time to spend with colleagues from other units to be sure of picking up all the opportunities, and the complexity of negotiations required to achieved standardisation prevented progress in a number of areas such as pack sizes and formulations. But the networking bias in Consco's approach was stopping it from taking the sort of central initiatives necessary to realise more of the available benefits. Changes in the approach to bolster networking with some more powerful central initiatives needed to be considered.

Synergy Killers

Two important synergy killers were identified. First and foremost, the personal incentive system needed to change. The historical belief in unit autonomy, coupled with the exclusive emphasis on performance against individual unit budget targets, was making it difficult for individuals to work with other units, unless there was a clear short-term pay-off to both sides. Longer-term collaboration projects and situations involving win-lose trade-offs were being neglected. A wider set of evaluation criteria for promotions and bonuses, which would give explicit recognition for personal contributions to co-ordination efforts that were beneficial to the group, was needed. Secondly, the corporate marketing staff, who had a potentially important role to play, were not seen as sufficiently expert or sensitive to sharp-end business needs. Their advice and interventions were therefore discounted out of hand. For the corporate parent to succeed with a more proactive approach to linkages, some strengthening of skills and changes in attitude amongst the corporate staff were needed.

Business definitions

There was a heated debate over the desirability of redefining the businesses to move away from national entities to larger regional blocks. Advocates of this redefinition argued, in particular, that supply chain rationalisation in Europe was vital, but would never proceed while national barons were defending their autonomous empires. Others claimed that the separate national identities were a vital strength that should be preserved, but that more co-operation across the boundaries was necessary. Their view was that more project working, new forms of information exchange, and a stronger role for the centre on selected issues would make the national units work together well enough to achieve the desired benefits.

A separate business-definition issue concerned a relatively small group of products, which was sold primarily to industrial and commercial customers rather than to the consumer market. The level of co-operation and sharing between the national units in this product group was unacceptably low, mainly because the senior managers in the units were primarily concerned with the consumer product groups and were therefore not giving much attention or priority to the industrial/commercial products. After discussion of the issue, a widespread consensus emerged that the industrial/commercial product group should be broken out as a separate pan-European business, with its own management team. This management team, which would be solely responsible for the business, would then be charged with optimising the performance of the business, including taking advantage of co-operation and sharing opportunities throughout Europe.

Successes and Failures

The mechanisms and processes with which dissatisfaction was highest were the budget planning process, with its associated personal incentives, and the ineffective corporate marketing staff. The narrow budget process, in particular, was seen as a root cause of insular attitudes. If planning discussions with the centre could give more attention to group-wide issues and long-term business developments, the context for linkage management would be improved. Specific initiatives were also worth considering to make more headway with several of the unrealised synergy opportunities.

On the other hand, managers recognised that piecemeal changes might conflict with the prevailing corporate culture; a systematic programme of communication and change would probably be necessary. This view was reinforced by one of the successes of recent years: a new product range that had been developed centrally, then rolled out internationally with a clearly defined marketing platform and strong support from the corporate CEO. Several managers felt that this showed that well-designed, professionally executed corporate initiatives were now welcomed by unit managers, despite their historical preference for autonomy. The key, however, was to convince the unit managers that proposed initiatives did take account of local needs and had determined support from top-level corporate managers.

Review

Exhibit 7.7 shows the conclusions reached about the effectiveness of
Consco's linkage approach in five-lenses format.

Exhibit 7.7   Effectiveness of Consco's synergy approach.

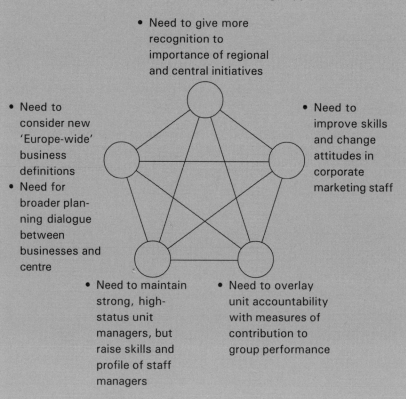

- Need to give more
  recognition to
  importance of regional
  and central initiatives

- Need to
  consider new
  'Europe-wide'
  business
  definitions
- Need for
  broader plan-
  ning dialogue
  between
  businesses and
  centre

- Need to
  improve skills
  and change
  attitudes in
  corporate
  marketing staff

- Need to maintain
  strong, high-
  status unit
  managers, but
  raise skills and
  profile of staff
  managers

- Need to overlay
  unit accountability
  with measures of
  contribution to
  group performance

Agenda for change

The output from the review should be a short-list of possible new initiatives for more detailed consideration. Since the review is a broadly based
stock take, the purpose is to create an agenda of possible changes, not to
arrive at firm conclusions about how to move forward. Each of the possible initiatives that emerge from the review will then need to be subjected
to the sort of detailed scrutiny described in Chapters 2–6.

The short-list should embrace:

- high priority unrealised synergy opportunities, including ways to address them;
- changes in underlying strategy or philosophy that may increase the effectiveness of the overall approach;
- changes in specific co-ordination processes or mechanisms, including elements that should be discontinued because they may be having a damaging effect, as well as new initiatives that should be considered;
- possible changes in business unit definitions.

Prioritisation of the ideas that emerge from the review is essential. The front-runners normally select themselves, either because of the size of the potential benefits (or disbenefits) or the strength of feeling among managers. But the cut-off on what to take forward is more a matter for judgement. We have four pieces of advice in forming the judgement.

First, be selective. A focused follow-through on three or four key initiatives is much more likely to yield tangible benefits than a long-drawn-out survey of a couple of dozen possibly attractive options. And if the review is not seen to lead on fairly quickly to action, its credibility will suffer and managers will lose enthusiasm.

Second, look forward, not back. Give preference to ideas that anticipate breaking trends and build links that will become increasingly valuable in the future. Avoid focusing on initiatives that deal with yesterday's problems or with issues that are likely to become less significant. Concentrate, for example, on putting in place pricing co-ordination mechanisms to avoid arbitrage in what will become an increasingly integrated European marketplace. Don't struggle to promote common design and manufacturing of components that more and more of the business units are already tending to outsource.

Third, use your rivals and competitors to guide your sense of priorities. If your main competitors are deriving much more benefit from sharing know-how than you are, move it up your priority list, unless there are good reasons why it is always likely to be less important to you than to them. If others have tried and failed with a shared-purchasing initiative, be cautious about pushing ahead with it. The concern should be with the specific achievements of known competitors, not with current general management fads and fashions. Of course, this presumes a certain level of competitive intelligence, which is not always present. However, we believe that efforts to find out about competitors' initiatives can play a valuable role in establishing a final short-list.

Fourth, recognise system effects. The five-lenses analysis brings out the connections between different aspects of the synergy approach. Successes and failures often stem from deeply rooted attitudes that underlie the use of certain mechanisms rather than others. Proposals to make changes in a given process or to address a specific opportunity may therefore entail consequential changes in other areas. Consider whether specific initiatives will work in the whole context in which they will be taken; assess the possibility that a systematic change programme to shift the overall culture may be required as a precondition for success in specific areas.

In the sidebar – 'Creating an agenda for possible changes in synergy parenting at Consco' – we complete our description of Consco's review of its co-ordination activities by showing what initiatives they decided to take further and why.

Creating an agenda for possible changes in synergy parenting at Consco

The review of Consco's synergy parenting generated a list of 26 possible initiatives to consider. To give some focus to the effort, these were narrowed down to six main areas for further investigation.

A 'Culture Change' Programme. The CEO of Consco concluded that the time was probably right, building on the findings of the review, to try to shift the culture away from its exclusive focus on unit autonomy towards a greater concern for group-wide strategy and results. He recognised that he would personally need to champion this initiative and to communicate his views widely. But he felt that managers in the units were now ready to accept a lead in this direction and recognised the importance of taking more advantage of synergies across the group. The general culture-change programme would need to be underpinned by specific changes in processes and mechanisms, and by initiatives to address specific co-ordination benefits. However, some shift in attitudes would be a precondition for success.

The Planning and Control Process. The CEO decided that he needed to look again at Consco's planning and control process. The shortcomings in the budget process, and in the associated personal incentives, had come over loud and clear. The directions of change, towards a greater emphasis on group issues and longer time horizons, were evident, but he was aware that there were dangers in moving away from the historical disciplines and motivation provided by the budget. He therefore embarked on a full review of Consco's budget and strategy planning processes, including their links to personal bonuses. He saw this as an integral part of the culture-change programme.

Coaching Roles of Regional Management and Staff. The review had shown that there probably was an unfulfilled role for the parent in helping to identify and promote certain linkages across the European region. Ways of strengthening the skills and resources of the regional team to help and coach the units needed to be considered. There were particular issues to address concerning the competence, attitudes and size of the regional marketing staff.

Supply Chain Project. An European supply chain and purchasing rationalisation project was set up, led by a senior executive from the European headquarters, but with participation from most of the main national units. The remit of the team was to look in detail both at the benefits available and at the options for realising them. The CEO made clear that he wanted the project team to look at possible organisation changes, including business redefinitions, as part of its remit.

Customer Relationships. A study of key account management was set up. It was led by a senior marketing executive from the regional team, who had recently been recruited from one of Consco's competitors. This executive had a number of ideas for key account management and co-ordination across Europe that he was keen to promote. However the CEO made sure that a cross section of experienced unit marketing managers participated in the team to carry out the study.

Training and Management Development. The group head of human resources was asked to lead another project team to look into the opportunities for more sharing on training and management development.

Given the trends in Consco's European businesses, the CEO felt that these were the priority areas to follow through in the first instance. As and when progress had been made on some of these issues, there were a variety of other less urgent opportunities and initiatives that he wanted to look into.

Practical guidance

Many companies are attracted by the idea of auditing how well their current linkage parenting is working. But such reviews are often unproductive and frustrating. It is all too easy for the review not to bring to the surface the changes that are really needed, to get bogged down in excessive detail, or to fail to create a realistic but innovative agenda for action. This is disillusioning for participants who resent the wasted time and energy and resolve not to do it again. To forestall this possibility, we end this chapter with a short summary of our tips for making a review worthwhile.

Tone

The tone of any review tends to be set by the chief executive. Managers try to discern what sort of answers the CEO is looking for when a review is announced. Does he/she want radical new ideas, or confirmation of current directions? Are there some changes that he/she is trying to steer towards? How open, and how open-minded, does he/she want us to be? Senior managers in the parent need to be aware of the messages that they wish to give to participants in the review, and the means by which to communicate them as clearly and unequivocally as possible.

Openness

Even if the tone is set to encourage openness, managers may not want to put their heads above the parapet. In companies with an open, no-blame culture this is less of an issue; elsewhere, getting dissident, counter-cultural or radical ideas on the table is often hard. In these circumstances, outsiders can play a useful role by gathering views confidentially, then feeding them back in a digested, unidentified form to senior managers. In this way, openness is encouraged but at minimal personal risk.

Sizing

In Chapter 2, we argued that sizing the benefit, assessing its order-of-magnitude value, is essential in deciding whether to intervene. Sizing is equally helpful for setting priorities in an overall review of linkage management. Although sizing the relative importance of different opportunities and initiatives is difficult, we believe that the attempt to quantify and cross-calibrate is the best way to ensure that the review focuses on things that can really make a difference.

80:20

Deciding what not to worry about is as important as deciding what to put on the short-list. The familiar 80:20 rule can help here. Concentrate on the issues that you are fairly sure represent big hits. Don't try to resolve all the uncertainties during the review. Be content with 80% of the right answer. A danger in any review is paralysis by analysis: the 80:20 rule is the best way to avoid this pitfall.

Follow-through

In many ways, the most important part of the review is what happens after it has been completed. The real pay-off comes from focused, in-depth analysis of the short-list of initiatives, followed by decisions about what to do. Without follow-through, no review can be worth the effort. The review framework we propose can be a useful way of filtering ideas into a promising short-list of options. But the benefits come from putting these options through the mental disciplines, and deciding whether and how to intervene.

Notes

1   See Michael Goold, Andrew Campbell and Marcus Alexander, *Corporate-level Strategy: Creating Value in the Multibusiness Company*, John Wiley & Sons, 1994, for a full description of these companies' synergy approaches.

2   See Michael Goold, Andrew Campbell and Marcus Alexander, *Corporate-level Strategy: Creating Value in the Multibusiness Company*, John Wiley & Sons, 1994, Chapter 12, for a fuller description of the five lenses analysis of parenting characteristics.

Epilogue

Our work on synergy over the last 10 years has taken us on a roller coaster intellectual journey. We started out in the 1980s thinking that we were going to find a link between different kinds of synergy and different kinds of mechanism: for example, we thought that economies of scale might be best achieved by centralisation and that vertical integration might be best achieved by liaison committees. However, most of these hypotheses have been disproved and we have realised that synergy interventions need to be crafted to meet the specifics of each situation. This book has therefore been designed to help managers to choose workable interventions to address particular synergy opportunities.

As an epilogue, it is worth reflecting on what we have learnt from the research. We will take three perspectives: the perspective of the parent manager, the perspective of the business unit manager and the perspective of received wisdom.

The parent's perspective

For parent managers trying to decide what to do about synergy in general and specific synergies in particular, we have learnt quite a few lessons.

1   Synergy opportunities can often be mirages. Each one needs to be considered carefully to confirm the size of the prize and the need to intervene.

2   Respect for the priorities and views of business unit managers is a
     good starting position. If business unit managers are not voluntarily
     working together or are resisting collaborative initiatives, parent
     managers need to understand why. The resistance is usually ra-
     tional from the business managers' perspective. If resistance is based
     on superior knowledge of the real costs and benefits, parent man-
     agers need to back off. Only if resistance is based on one of the four
     categories of parenting opportunity do parent managers have a rea-
     son for intervening.

3   There are many different ways in which any particular synergy can
     be created, so there are no 'right' ways of intervening. Instead,
     parent managers need to think through a range of possible options,
     and pick the one that is likely to work in that particular circum-
     stance.

4   Parent managers need to be humble about their own skills and
     their ability to develop new skills. Most synergy interventions work
     well when they are championed by someone with the appropriate
     skill set. If that person doesn't exist, it is often better to go for a less
     ambitious prize rather than risk bodging the job.

5   Organisations are a complex bundle of competencies, relationships,
     processes and values. When trying to change behaviour, it is neces-
     sary to think about the whole bundle, i.e. the impact a particular
     intervention will have on the organisation as a whole. It is not pos-
     sible to isolate one behaviour and design interventions that affect
     only that behaviour. What's more, organisations are chaotic and
     react in ways that can never be fully predicted. This means that all
     interventions involve some downside risks. A balance therefore
     needs to be maintained between commitment to seeing an inter-
     vention through and willingness to be flexible if unforeseen
     problems arise.

6   Organisations are not always natural homes for synergy. In fact valu-
     able relationships between businesses are often easier when they
     involve independent companies dealing at arms length. Parent
     managers can therefore make a big contribution by eliminating
     'synergy killers', aspects of their organisation which actively dis-
     courage business units from working together.

The business manager's perspective

For business unit managers continually looking for opportunities to create value and often bombarded with requests from the corporate centre to co-operate, we have also learned important lessons.

1   Synergy is not about a free-ride where one business unit is getting free help or a cross-subsidy from another unit or from the parent. Business units that are only interested in the benefits they get out of so-called synergies and ignore the legitimate interests of those with whom they are collaborating will undermine the spirit of co-operation on which genuine synergies depend. There is in synergy, as in every other field, no free lunch. Business unit managers should expect to pay for favours they receive, in cash, in kind or in IOUs for future favours that will flow in the opposite direction.

2   Synergy is not about submerging the interests of one business unit for the good of the whole. If there is a pile of gold to be released as a result of some linkage, it ought to be possible for all participants to gain a piece of it. If one business is going to suffer as a result of the link, the managers of that business need to make the costs absolutely clear, so that they can be taken into account in the total equation.

There will be occasions when a synergy involves a win/lose outcome where it is hard to compensate the loser. If these synergies are to proceed, they will have to be pushed through by parent managers. In such cases, the parent managers have to make the judgement call about how important the synergies are. Business managers can help by laying out the true benefits and costs; but should beware of playing God. They may not be in the best position to decide what the balance of cost and benefit is.

3   Synergy is about mutual interest or, as the Mars Principles call it, 'Mutuality'. Business unit managers should be looking out for ways to create value through working with any other business, whether it is a sister company or a third party. The only difference in attitude to sister companies is a more relaxed approach to how the cake is divided. If there is an opportunity to do a favour for a sister company at low cost, do it. Business unit interests should be put

first, but don't let this be an excuse for being mean to the rest of the 'family'.

4   Synergies often work best without the presence of a parent. When two business unit managers can see the pot of gold, believe it is large, and are motivated to go for it, they are normally better left to themselves. They can figure out what to do to get the benefit and how to divide up the spoils without external help. In fact, co-operative spirit is often dampened just by the presence of a parent: the stakes are higher, there is a danger that the parent will intervene in negotiations, and there is a third party to be kept informed raising the costs of co-operation.

5   Recognise that there are, however, some situations in which the parent has a role to play. Unexploited synergy opportunities can exist because business unit managers cannot see or figure out how to get the benefit. In these cases they need to be willing to be led by parent managers or sister units into links that release the gold. In some situations, the parent managers may even have to impose a decision on all the units involved.

But how do business unit managers decide whether they are being led towards a lake of gold or a mirage? The answer is that it depends on their assessment of the expertise of the leader. If the business unit managers judge that the leader's expertise is high, they should put aside scepticism. If not, they should fight their corner until the benefits are made clear.

The received wisdom perspective

The final perspective from which to view synergy is that of received wisdom. What commonly held views about synergy have we disproved and what views have we reinforced?

Many writers and consultants have argued that the difficulty companies have been having with synergy is due to a lack of managerial sophistication. One of the most articulate is Sumantra Ghoshal, who describes the issue as one of third generation business problems being addressed with second generation organisation structures and first generation management skills.

We understand and have sympathy with Ghoshal's views: many synergies cannot be released because the parenting skills do not match the opportunity. But often the difficulty is caused by other factors: the synergy is a mirage, the prize is not large enough, the risk of negative knock-on effects is too great. By telling mangers that the problem is one of skill and effort, the 'try harder school' is not telling the whole story and, in some cases, could make things worse rather than better.

Another commonly held view we are uncomfortable with is the anti-SBU proposition. Many writers, most notably Gary Hamel, have argued that the reason why synergy is difficult is that companies have decentral-ised to self-contained business units (SBUs). This, they argue, creates barriers between SBUs that are difficult to overcome.

At one level this proposition is a tautology. Since synergy involves creating links between SBUs, any attempt to set up isolated SBUs with no links is going to reduce synergy.

At another level, however, the proposition is wrong. It is not neces-sary to eliminate the identity and focus of self-contained business units in order to promote synergy. Synergy is possible between SBUs. We have found many examples of focused SBUs that have co-operated fa-mously in pursuit of mutually beneficial synergy opportunities. Indeed, the spur of stretching SBU performance targets is a prime reason for their managers to seek out synergy opportunities. Furthermore, lack of clarity about SBU definitions is often a major cause of synergy difficulties, since managers become uncertain about the extent of their responsibilities.

Problems do arise, however, if SBU managers are excessively focused on their own businesses, to the point where they are unwilling to work with other SBUs. Also, if SBU boundaries are cast in concrete, they will be hard to change in response to shifting competitive realities and may be less amenable to co-operation across the boundaries.

We therefore feel that a compromise proposition is likely to give the best guidance to managers. Clear, well-defined SBUs are a valuable build-ing block in multi-business companies. However, if SBU boundaries are viewed as battlements that need defending rather than co-operative frontiers that may need parenting, synergy will be damaged.

A third commonly held view is that synergy problems are due, in the main, to the not-invented-here (NIH) attitudes of business unit manag-ers. Our research has led us to see the issue from the other end of the telescope. Synergy problems, in our view, are more often caused by misguided parent managers than by belligerent business unit heads. We recognise that business unit managers are often blinkered, but so are parent managers. Moreover, a blinkered view is not the same as NIH. In fact NIH in its purest form – the business unit manager can see the opportunity but doesn't want to change to a better alternative because it has been developed by someone else – is rare. Most resistance comes from business unit managers who don't want to change because they think the change will be for the worse. Parent managers, we believe, are unlikely to make wise synergy decisions unless they understand the issue from the business unit managers' perspective.

In contrast to the commonly held views that we want to see adjusted, we are in wholehearted agreement with those who believe synergy can be a source of competitive advantage. Most writers on strategy have pointed out the potential for multi-business companies to gainan advantage over their rivals through good synergy management. Most have also pointed out the high failure rate. Those who succeed, they argue, will have a huge advantage.

We support this view. Synergy management can be a major source of advantage. 3M, ABB, Canon, Mars and Unilever can all credit some of their market place success to their special abilities at managing synergy. Moreover, the bar is being raised all the time. As multi-business companies become more focussed, the competition between them has become less about choosing which businesses to support and more about driving extra value from the businesses they own. Synergy is a superb way of doing this.

But synergy is not essential. Multi-business companies can be successful without it. Companies like KKR, Virgin, Emerson and Granada create value as a result of the direct influence of the corporate centre and have very few, if any, links between business units. So synergy is a source of competitive advantage, but it is not the only source of advantage for multi-business companies.

In summary, we believe we have developed a distinctive view of synergy and have learned valuable lessons about this complex topic. The bottom line is that well managed synergy can be a golden prize where additional value is created from the same resources. But badly managed, synergy can destroy value, undermine self confidence and lead managers in the wrong direction. The four mental disciplines that form the bulk of this book should help managers get the best from their synergy efforts. They will help managers avoid mirages and implementation disasters and find those lakes of extra value that can be profitably tapped.

Index